I loved this book. It both moved me to te
will forever color the way I see life. I higl
part of Shemaiah Gonzalez's revolution o

Sally Read, edit

Imagine joy as a glass of bubbly champagne, and here's your friend Shemaiah, inviting you to drink up. She doesn't write about a cheap, easy joy. Hers is hard-earned, the kind you take hold of and cherish because you know its value. This kind of joy she offers, it left me wanting more of it in my own life too.

Traci Rhoades, author of *Not All Who Wander (Spiritually) Are Lost* and *Shaky Ground*

Undaunted Joy must have been a joy to write. It is a joy to read. For one, Shemaiah Gonzalez knows that you can find joy in the new, improved garbage bag. You can find it in both "the mundane and the magnificent"—the adjacent, empty airline seat on an international flight, a car wash, your favorite pants, a Costco trip, naps, and daydreaming! Gonzalez knows what the psalmist knows: We sometimes need more than even family and friends to get us through pain, suffering, a pandemic, spiritual warfare, terror attacks, doubt, and death itself. We need faith in a living and loving Father who offers us transcendent, undaunted joy.

John Poch, professor of English and creative writing, Grace College

It's rare to come across a book that so thoroughly embodies its own message. Shemaiah Gonzalez's study of joy is a joy: to read, to engage, to behold. Her clear-eyed insistence on choosing all that is good—and offering unapologetic resistance to the demands of evil—cuts through every false complication to reveal the beautiful truth at the core of things. Let her show you how to do the same.

Katy Carl, author of *As Earth Without Water* and *Fragile Objects*

Shemaiah Gonzalez's deliciously poetic debut book, *Undaunted Joy*, is ripe with delight. Some may think of joy as a naive, indulgent refusal to deal with the wounded world. Doesn't joy see? But this is the entire point, says Gonzalez, as she invites readers to behold God's world and squeal their pleasure. To meet Gonzalez in these pages is to long for her joy—and the hopeful faith that makes it possible.

Jen Pollock Michel, award-winning author of *In Good Time* and *Surprised by Paradox*

These charming meditations remind us to deepen our awareness of the ordinary wonders that surround us always. Shemaiah Gonzalez does not deny the presence of difficulty or sorrow but offers moments of joy as a companion to the ups and downs of life. This book inspires a brightened sense of the sacred in all things that will bring more delight to our days and our world.

Lyanda Lynn Haupt, author of *Rooted*

The "gracious fading light of sunset," homemade quilts, and freshly cut grass are only a few of the many inspirations for joy that Shemaiah Gonzalez details in this beautiful book. But as cozy and reassuring as these reflections are, *Undaunted Joy* isn't an invitation to gloss over or deny our own or the world's pain, loss, and suffering. Rather, Gonzalez invites readers to experience joy as an antidote to anxiety and despair. When you reach the last page, may you—as was true for me—be persuaded that joy isn't a luxury but, truly, a necessity and a way of life.

Jennifer Grant, author of *Dimming the Day* and *Finding Calm in Nature*

My favorite sentence in Shemaiah Gonzalez's *Undaunted Joy* is "He wanted to paint joy." It might surprise you to know that she's writing about Van Gogh and his art. That's what Gonzalez does with this book. She can take a person almost universally known as a symbol of desperation and see the brightness in him. We live in fraught times—we've always lived in fraught times—but Gonzalez teaches us that people have always found their way to joy.

Sherman Alexie, author of National Book Award winner *The Absolutely True Diary of a Part-Time Indian*

The call to joy from Job to Jack Gilbert and Chuang Tzu to Ross Gay runs through world faith traditions, world poetry, and the lives of saints and sages as one of our greatest antidotes to despair. In this quiet, family-oriented, often humorous book, Shemaiah Gonzalez has boarded that good ship. May its voyages grow in number and never end.

David James Duncan, author of *Sun House* and *The Brothers K*

undaunted *joy*

undaunted *joy*

The REVOLUTIONARY ACT *of* CULTIVATING DELIGHT

SHEMAIAH GONZALEZ

ZONDERVAN REFLECTIVE

Undaunted Joy

Published in Grand Rapids, Michigan, by Zondervan. Zondervan is a registered trademark of The Zondervan Corporation, L.L.C., a wholly owned subsidiary of HarperCollins Christian Publishing, Inc.

Requests for information should be addressed to customercare@harpercollins.com.

Zondervan titles may be purchased in bulk for educational, business, fundraising, or sales promotional use. For information, please email SpecialMarkets@Zondervan.com.

Library of Congress Cataloging-in-Publication Data

Names: Gonzalez, Shemaiah, 1974- author.
Title: Undaunted joy : the revolutionary act of cultivating delight / Shemaiah Gonzalez.
Description: Grand Rapids, Michigan : Zondervan Reflective, [2025] | Includes bibliographical references,
Identifiers: LCCN 2024047444 (print) | LCCN 2024047445 (ebook) | ISBN 9780310163176 (softcover) | ISBN 9780310163190 (ebook) | ISBN 9780310163206 (audio)
Subjects: LCSH: Joy—Religious aspects—Christianity | Christian women—Religious life. | BISAC: RELIGION / Christian Living / Inspirational | LITERARY COLLECTIONS / Essays
Classification: LCC BV4647.J68 G656 2025 (print) | LCC BV4647.J68 (ebook) | DDC 248.4—dc23/eng/20241125
LC record available at https://lccn.loc.gov/2024047444
LC ebook record available at https://lccn.loc.gov/2024047445

Published in association with the literary agency of WordServe Literary Group, Ltd., www.wordserveliterary.com.

Cover design: Thinkpen Design
Cover photo: © Danielle Donders/GettyImages
Interior design: Sara Colley

Printed in the United States of America

25 26 27 28 29 LBC 5 4 3 2 1

To my husband, Justo, and our sons, Massimo and Tomás

♬ *You make me so very happy; I'm so glad you came into my life.* ♬

contents

introduction

Man is fond of counting his troubles, but he
does not count his joys. If he counted them up
as he ought to, he would see that every lot has
enough happiness provided for it.
—Fyodor Dostoevsky, *Notes from Underground*

My mother told me my first word was *happy*.

I was sitting in my highchair when I said it. My face was covered with some sort of homemade mush she made with a food mill. I clapped my hands and declared, "Happy."

Perhaps I said "happy" because I liked the taste of the baby food, whether squash or apple or dare I say peas. Or maybe I was happy being there with my mother—basking in her attention and her love. Perhaps I was mimicking a song we sang at the little hippie church we attended in Southern California: *Happy are the people whose God is the Lord*. Or maybe it was all of these, or none of these and I didn't know what the word meant at all.

Perhaps it means I am predisposed to joy. Joy is a part of who I am because the Spirit has marked my heart, embossing me with his love, defining me.

Today I dwell in joy. But it was a long, tenuous road to get here.

My childhood was filled with poverty, abuse, and neglect. I spent my teen years desperately attempting to flee that world and find my own. When I finally settled down, married, and held the stability and love I had always longed for, I collapsed. For the first time, I wasn't grappling for my daily basic needs. In a safe place, with my husband caring and providing for me, trauma overwhelmed me. There were days when I couldn't leave the house, dress myself, or even get out of bed.

Looking back, I see three moments that moved me out of that place.

The first is quite mundane. I would have missed it had I not quoted the moment many times since and recalled where the words came from.

One evening, early in our marriage, my husband and I had a neighbor over for dinner. After the meal, as we washed the dishes and wiped the crumbs off the counters, our neighbor offered to take out the trash. As he tied up the old bag, I pulled out a replacement and nearly squealed with delight when I realized I was going to use the new trash bags I had bought. Reinforced with ForceFlex technology(!), these new bags promised to prevent leaks and splits. *And* they smelled good! My reaction was a little over the top. I quickly saw myself through my husband's and neighbor's eyes. My enthusiasm was as if I were on camera, in a commercial for trash bags.

I felt myself turn red. Hot and embarrassed, I turned down the volume on my zeal. The neighbor, without skipping a beat, walked out the door with the old bag heaving and said, "You have to get excited about these little things. The big stuff doesn't happen that often, and when it does, it's usually something bad."

That line sizzled in my brain for a while.

It was true. Most of the big moments in my life—college graduation, falling in love, marriage—were all behind me. I had been living my life thinking, "I'll be happy when X, Y, Z happens." Now they had all happened. And I wasn't really happy. How was I to exist moving forward? Was this all there was?

To be honest, I don't even remember that neighbor's name anymore. It was twenty years ago. He made the comment in passing and probably didn't even think about it. But these words would become a touchstone I'd hold on to.

The second moment happened in therapy. I had become so anxious I could barely breathe. Trauma from my childhood came out sideways. After years of not being allowed to have many emotions, I didn't know how to emote. Weekly, I went to cognitive therapy sessions where I learned basics, like how to breathe, that anger was an emotion I needed to learn to express, and how to break down seemingly unbearable tasks into smaller steps.

It was slow, grueling work.

One day when—I now presume—I had made enough progress and was getting a little comfortable, I slopped down in the therapist's chair ready to unload my latest story of woe. The therapist listened as she had before, but this time, when I finished, she repeated my story back to me—as a comedy.

She told me the very same story of interpersonal

miscommunication and relational mishaps as if it were a Thursday night sitcom on NBC.

It could have *not* worked. She took a huge risk with this approach. It could have fallen flat and left me feeling unsupported and more vulnerable. But it didn't. I heard what she was trying to tell me. My life was good and full and rich—and hysterically funny. I had been so focused on what wasn't quite right that I couldn't appreciate the joy all around me.

It took a while to rewire my thoughts, but that afternoon, my therapist gave me a glimpse of how to repair the cracked lens I was watching my life through.

The third moment was a big one, and it was bad.

In 2005, my second year of marriage, my childhood best friend crawled into her bathtub, fully clothed, swallowed a bottle of pills, and then placed a plastic bag over her head to make certain she would succeed in what she set out to do.

When I got the call, I wasn't surprised. We hadn't spoken in a year, mainly because we were both too fragile to help each other. I was a mess. She was a mess. In the years prior, I had prolonged her life, several times. It had gotten to the point where I wasn't sure I could help her and keep myself above water too.

After that fateful call, I knew I couldn't give in to the darkness any longer. If I did, her fate would become my own. I whispered, "Lord, help my unbelief." It was the only prayer I could truly pray. I believed in God, but I didn't believe I would get any better. I didn't believe he would heal me.

But he did. I can't explain how it happened. Or how it continues to happen. I prayed that I'd trust him and I started focusing on the small stuff.

Along the way, I discovered I suffocated joy. It was difficult to accept kindness or affection from friends or even my husband. When joy crept up on me, it felt akin to anxiety and sent me into a panic. I ran away from delight and glee and pleasure. I knew how to operate in sadness or survival mode. It was all I knew. But *joy* felt foreign.

Nearly a decade ago, I read the novel *Family Life* by Akhil Sharma. It tells a story of an immigrant family from India. The parents dream of a better life for their sons in the States. They place most of their hope in their oldest son, a teenager, brilliant and beautiful with an auspicious life ahead of him. A freak accident occurs as he dives into a swimming pool, and he suffers severe and irreversible brain damage. The family's hope for the American dream is spent on caring for this vegetative young man, and the younger son falls through the cracks. His mother disappears into the care of her oldest son, and his father withdraws into alcoholism. As the younger son spends most of his time caring for his brother, he longs for attention and affection from his parents. I spent most of the week I read this book crying along with the characters.

But the last few pages haunt me. The younger son overcomes. He acquires an education, secures a promising job, and finds love with a beautiful fiancée. And as he lies with her in the sunshine on the beach during, perhaps, his first vacation ever, he realizes he is happy—and this frightens him.

This is how the novel ends: with the frightening prospect of joy.

I knew this feeling intimately, but by the time I read the novel, I had moved past this fear. Just as my therapist taught me to emote anger—an emotion I had never been allowed to experience—by stomping my feet like a toddler whenever I felt the emotion come upon me, I also learned how to experience joy.

I had lived in survival mode for such a long time, waiting for the next crisis to happen, that I wouldn't allow myself a bit of happiness. Joy felt like an indulgence. Sometimes it even felt dangerous.

Slowly, I learned to see joy not as an indulgence but as a necessity. As a way of life. This didn't happen all at once, but through a slow process over time—one that continues even today.

Joy is not anxiety. As I welcomed it into my life, I learned to sit with it. I learned to say aloud, "I'm happy," to remind myself that it was not anxiety, that joy was not something to fear.

Songs from that little hippie church my parents attended when I was small resurface in my mind often. (If one ever wonders if it even matters that you take a small child to church, who can't participate and is probably not even listening, I am living proof that it does matter.) I heard Scripture and songs whispered that have sustained me throughout my life. They were building blocks that established a strong base to build my own faith upon. One song line that comes back to me when I think about joy is "The joy of the Lord is your strength." I can't even remember the entire song, just the refrain, over and over again.

It comes from a verse in the book of Nehemiah. After seventy long years in Babylonian exile, the Israelites returned to their land, shell-shocked. They felt guilty for the lack of faith that had put them in exile to begin with. They were weeping and mourning when the prophet Nehemiah gave them a word from the Lord: "Do not grieve, for the joy of the LORD is your strength."[1]

He told them to cook a feast to celebrate the rebuilding of the wall around the temple. The message was clear: It was time to live joyously.

Maybe like the Israelites, or to a much lesser degree, like me, you have suffered. Maybe you don't feel like you can be joyful, don't know how to, don't deserve to.

Joy can follow suffering. We should not be frightened of it. Rather, walking through joy and suffering allows us to see the disparity between the two.

How do we build a life that allows us to be happy? You wouldn't tell a child not to be happy, would you? Neither does our Father in heaven. He wants to give us good things.

There is a call to joy in the air. To declare goodness. To cement it. To show others how to see again. To give them permission to experience joy.

In the titular scene from the 1952 musical *Singin' in the Rain*, Gene Kelly's character realizes he's in love. It's raining, but he waves the cab driver on and begins to sing and dance in the downpour. He sings his joy to everyone he encounters, and, in the film's iconic shot, he stands with outstretched arms, his face tilted up toward the rain as he sings, "Come on with the rain, I've a smile on my face." It used to be difficult for me to watch. That one frame was too much to see. I teared up with that frame—the unadulterated, undaunted joy.

I can look at it now. I can allow myself to feel that sort of happiness at trash bags or a good cup of coffee or a view of the ocean or the fact that capybaras exist.

I never would have called myself an authority on joy, but perhaps being willing to look at joy, to not be afraid of it, does make me an authority. Perhaps showing others how to see it will make joy contagious.

In her poem "Welcome Morning," Anne Sexton shares the delights of the morning: towel and brush, a "chapel of eggs," and "holy birds at the kitchen window." She thanks God for all of it, for it is him showing up in the quotidian of her morning. She ends the poem with a reminder to herself to notice this presence, to say it aloud, for "Joy that isn't shared, I've heard, dies young."[2]

Joy doesn't have to be something big. It is the small stuff that builds a joy-filled life. God is there in those moments. It is easier to see those moments when I am close to God, for joy is the fruit of knowing him. I see joy clearly when I allow him to open my eyes. When I share joy with others. And when I let him, his joy, be my strength.

In the pages ahead, I'll share some stories with you. Perhaps these stories, of finding joy in laundry and Van Gogh's paintings of sunflowers, in daydreaming, and even in the darkest of places, will allow you to see life anew. Perhaps you will, like me, no longer wait for the big things to happen but will find there is abundance today. Each day holds joy in the mundane and the magnificent—we just need to learn to see.

1

of naps

Nearly every single day, after lunch, I take a nap in my chair, like an old lady.

I say "old lady" because my grandmother napped in a mammoth brown recliner in her den. This often happened after she watched her "stories." I'd walk in, and her head would be tilted back in all sorts of unnaturalness, her mouth gaping open, drool pooling on her shoulder like the basin of a waterfall.

Because I was young and thought she was very, very old and might be dead (even though it embarrasses me to say this, she was not much older than I am today, and let me tell you, I'm in my *prime*), I'd whisper, "Nana, are you asleep?"

She would startle awake and deny it all, *straight to my face*, even as she wiped the line of slobber off her chin: "Nah, I was only resting my eyes!"

As a child, I didn't comprehend the need for naps. In preschool, the teachers had us lie on the floor on diminutive, colorful mats for nap time. I'd lie there staring at the ceiling, counting the little holes in the tiles, until a teacher would come over and tell me to stop singing. I had no idea I had been singing. But I must have been. I had to do something instead of lying there wasting time. My mind couldn't stop thinking.

When my teachers realized I could read, they let me lie down with a book while the others slept. This is when I started to look forward to nap time. I could catch up on my reading.

I've heard it said that youth is wasted on the young—that is even more true of naps.

I don't have a recliner like my Nana, but I do have a blue midcentury modern armchair in my office. It isn't the most comfortable chair to nap in, and this might be the point. I put a throw pillow on the arm of the chair and sort of slump over, like a marionette without anyone at the strings. I don't want a deep slumber. I want a rest long enough to reset but short enough to not wake cranky.

To ensure this sort of snooze (and I have discovered that twenty-five minutes is the sweet spot), I have a particular setup.

1. Turn on a fan. If I am too warm, too comfortable, I'll sleep too long. I make the room cool so I will have to wake.
2. Draw the shades. My office is at the front of the house, near the front door. I do not want the Amazon delivery guy to peak in and see me drooling on my throw pillow.
3. Set a backup alarm in case I sleep too long.

Since I am a writer, I imagine myself, like *Mad Men*'s Don Draper (without the heavy drinking and philandering), needing a snooze because I have been so incredibly creative that I need to find more ideas in my afternoon reveries.

But the truth is, I'm an intense person. Sometimes I am so intense it exhausts even me. I can't imagine how much I must exasperate my family and closest friends—or the person at the gym, store, or school who doesn't love me like family.

I have a lot going on in my head. Not all of it is creative. In fact, most of it is stupid. So I take a nap each day to slow my heart rate, to make sure I don't have a heart attack, to *calm the heck down*!

I am inordinately blissful when I burrow into my armchair for my afternoon doze. I am so grateful I have the space and time to nap and that I have learned that I need this time to reset. As I close my eyes, I pray, "Lord, I know you are going to make everything better."

Poet Wendell Berry has a marvelous collection of what he calls "Sabbath poems," poems that speak to that longing for rest in body and spirit. A line in one of these poems stays with me: "Sleep is the prayer the body prays."[1] I feel that line in my bones. And I feel it each afternoon when I have let myself spin into emails, texts, to-do lists, and the thoughts in my head that run rampant. I know it is time to pause and let my body pray.

Years ago, when I was in seminary, our cohort had a weekend retreat. I was looking forward to it. The retreat was to be held at a cabin in the woods, with trails and fireplaces and my classmates and deep conversations. As a starving student, I thought of this as a vacation. Yet when I arrived, I found myself so exhausted, I could only attend the mandatory sessions. Otherwise, I slept. I approached my professor, Dr. Blom, and offered my apologies. Dr. Blom was the dreamiest seminary professor. He was kind and charitable. He read books outside of theology texts and sometimes wore dashing black turtlenecks. He reminded me of the dad from the 1960s television show *Gidget*. That dad was a professor too, an English professor at UCLA. Gidget's dad and Dr. Blom are what I imagined good fathers to be like. So I wasn't surprised at Dr. Blom's answer to my apology.

He reminded me that when Elijah was running from Jezebel, who wanted to kill him, the Lord had Elijah take a nap. "God understands naps, Shemaiah," he told me. "Sometimes when you sense his presence, all you can do is rest in it."

Dr. Blom was exactly right. I felt *at peace*. It was a new feeling to me. It was unfamiliar. It was so *delicious*, sort of intoxicating. All I wanted to do was soak in it.

There is a sense of surrender in a nap, especially in my midday naps. Wendell Berry captures that sense of surrender in his Sabbath poems:

> The body in the invisible
> Familiar room accepts the gift
> Of sleep, and for a while is still;
> Instead of will, it lives by drift[2]

Naps are my prayer, to give up my will; for God to reset me, my intensity, my heart, my spirit; to redirect me to his will. To redirect my life *by drift*.

So I put head to pillow and surrender to that luxurious, delicious . . . peace.

2

joy as an act of defiance

It is one of those bleak and grimsome nights when you can't see your hand in front of your face. One of those nights when you fear death is very near. For it is. It is 1917, in a dank, rat-infested trench on the Western Front somewhere in France.

Trench warfare marked most of the fighting in World War I, and on the Western Front, no significant advances were made by either side. Years of attacks and counterattacks were costly. The Battle of Verdun alone saw over seven hundred thousand casualties. These men were inundated with artillery fire, barbed wire, poison gas, and the bleak conditions of the trenches.

Here, by the light of his cigarette, British soldier Isaac Rosenberg penned a poem that has haunted me through the years.

Sombre the night is:
And, though we have our lives, we know
What sinister threat lurks there.

Dragging these anguished limbs, we only know
This poison-blasted track opens on our camp—
On a little safe sleep.

Rosenberg is grounded in reality in that trench. How could he not be? He is well aware of the danger that lurks beyond his earthen walls. Writing poetry in such a setting is already a bold and courageous feat, but Rosenberg doesn't stop there.

But hark! Joy—joy—strange joy.
Lo! Heights of night ringing with unseen larks:
Music showering on our upturned listening faces.

Death could drop from the dark
As easily as song—
But song only dropped.[1]

Rosenberg finds joy in the middle of a wasteland. And when he hears it, in the form of a lark's song, he does not dismiss it or brush it off as a chance or fluke. He grabs hold of it, with his upturned face, as an act of resistance. Joy is a life buoy in the midst of misery. Rosenberg will not be broken.

The poem is reminiscent of a psalm. This is no coincidence. Rosenberg was Jewish, and although he grew up in London's East End, his poetry drips with the pastoral references of the Psalms and is steeped in the inner cadence of his childhood.

In the psalms of lament, there is a pivot, a moment in which the psalmist turns away from sorrow and toward God's goodness and sovereignty. Here too, in Rosenberg's poem, he turns away from his obvious anguish. He could have stayed mired in despair, but he chooses to turn toward the transcendent. And it's as if joy is God himself, present in a lark's song.

○ ○ ○

There are days when my alarm sounds in the morning and I feel as if something is sitting on my chest. This something hates me. It breathes into my neck and whispers all my fears and weaknesses, those real and those perceived, and it hisses out-and-out lies into my ear, to make certain I do not see any goodness in the day before me.

This is when I know I must find joy quickly. Where is it present in that very moment? In my home? In my schedule in the day before me? Or is it present in hope, lingering in the future?

In his book *Surprised by Joy*, C. S. Lewis writes of moments throughout his life when he found joy. When he became a Christian, he realized that all those moments of joy happened when God was present. Joy was when God was pursuing him through imagination, education, and relationships. Lewis equated joy with God himself.

In my mornings of despair and depression, I must notice God's presence, fast. Where is he pursuing me in joy, even amid the anguished attack? Unlike Peter, who begins to sink when he takes his eyes off Jesus, I must keep my eyes on him.[2]

I felt this way during the first few weeks of the COVID-19 pandemic in March 2020. I live in Seattle, where the first wave of the pandemic hit. I was in the car on errands when I heard the news that we would be going into lockdown for the next two weeks. I pulled over and texted a friend in state government.

"Does this mean I should go to Costco and load up?"

He texted back, "I think that would be a good idea."

The normally raucous Costco was quiet. I moved silently among hundreds of shoppers filling their carts with meat and canned goods and toilet paper. Fear overwhelmed me as I gripped the cart handle.

"Where are you?" I prayed.

It didn't take long. I found him present in the eyes of a little girl. She sat in the front of a cart, in one of the double infant seats. Her doll sat in the seat next to her. Shoppers were tense and frantic, but she sat there with her doll, brushing its hair and holding its hand, like the calm within the storm.

Without thinking, I broke the silence around me and burst into laughter. I laughed at the absurdity of it all. The little girl saw me smile and smiled back, oblivious to the panic around.

In my heart I heard, "Do you think this surprises me? This is nothing new. Keep your eyes on me."

○ ○ ○

In the days that followed, it was difficult to find my footing. All the markers in my daily routine, connections, and institutions were gone. I found myself waking in a panic in the dark hours of the morning before the day had even begun.

"Where are you in this?" I prayed again one morning a few days later. I did not want to get out of bed, but I also couldn't return to sleep.

I heard, "Go to the water."

Lake Washington, a mammoth thirty-plus-square-mile lake, is a fifteen-minute walk from my house. I pulled on some joggers and sneakers and started out to the lake. In my soul, I was daring God to show up. I don't know what I was expecting, but it was as if I were telling God, "You better show up! Everything is a mess. And now you got me out of bed. Just do something!"

The sky was still steely blue when I arrived at the lake. I watched a man make his way down to the dock with a flashlight and a fishing pole. A pair of geese walked by with five goslings in tow.

"This is pleasant," I thought, "but still not good enough to get out of bed. Not enough to fix the world."

I looked across the lake to the city of Bellevue, ten miles away. Its skyscrapers were still lit for the night. Behind the city stood the Cascade Mountain Range, solid and constant. The mountains seemed illuminated by the snow still draped upon them.

Then I noticed the light around me had changed. Steely-blue turned to indigo purple, then azure, and as the sun peeked over the mountains, streams of pink poured across the sky. When the sun reached its crest over the mountains, orange met pink radiating against whipped-cream clouds. I understood the meaning of the word *breathtaking*, for I could not breathe.

I looked across the panorama before me and understood: This is what God does each day. He's done it for centuries, millennia. He is still in charge. The sun will still rise each morning.

The psalmist sings,

> Who stilled the roaring of the seas,
> the roaring of their waves
> and the turmoil of the nations
> The whole earth is filled with awe at your wonders;
> where morning dawns, where evening fades,
> You call forth songs of joy[3]

And me? I am to notice. I am to look for goodness and beauty and joy in the world. That is him, there, working and moving in the midst of it all. To see it, when others choose not to, when others cling to fear or even evil—that is an act of defiance.

○ ○ ○

On December 8, 1941, the day after the attack on Pearl Harbor, Japanese forces in occupied China took over a Christian boarding school called Chefoo. The school had been established sixty years prior to teach children of British and American missionaries and diplomats. First interned in an abandoned compound, these 252 students and teachers were eventually marched into Weihsien Internment Camp.[4]

Although the teachers, most of whom were not much older than the students, knew of the atrocities in Nanking, where Japanese soldiers went door-to-door systematically raping and killing tens of thousands of Chinese civilians, they knew they needed to stay focused on Christ. They taught their students to do the same. As they walked into the camp, they sang together, "God is our refuge and strength. In times of trouble, we will not be afraid."[5] Mary Previte was twelve at the time and remembers that even though guards with guns and attack dogs surrounded them, she did not feel afraid. "Why would I be afraid when I knew God was nigh?" she would later recall.[6]

The children were taught to stay resolute. They were taught to look for joy. They would remain polite and cheerful no matter what. Food was scarce. They were always on the brink of starvation. Prisoners were fed boiled animal grain meant for livestock and ground eggshells to eat for extra calcium, but teachers reminded the students to have manners, not to slouch when they ate, to sing and not to stop smiling. They were to continue to live with dignity and grace.

The winter was freezing. No heat was provided. The children collected coal shavings from the guards' quarters. Shavings were mixed with dust and water and dried in the sun to create fuel. Teachers made it a game, gathering shavings with a bucket brigade and making a competition of which team could turn the potbellied stove red.

They should have been overpowered by the deprivation and evil around them, but they were not. Rather, this group of Christian children made a difference in the culture of the camp. They lived like this for four years until American paratroopers liberated them.

They were not oblivious to the dangers around them. They were taught to find joy, and they chose to live in it. Their teachers knew they would be lost without it. It is a formidable testimony to the power of joy as a weapon against the forces of evil. "Don't misunderstand me. I'm not saying this was Fun City," Mary Previte recalled years later. "I'm telling you; we lived a miracle where grownups preserved our childhood."[7]

○ ○ ○

In the book of Acts, when Paul and Silas were stripped, flogged, and thrown into prison with shackles fastened to their feet, they sang. They sang until a violent earthquake overcame them and the foundations of the prison were shaken. Even though their chains were loosened, they did not escape. Seeing this, the jailer came to believe in God and released them.

Years later, when Paul was in his sixties on house arrest, awaiting an uncertain future on the whims of the monstrous Roman emperor Nero, he decided to write a letter on joy: Philippians. Without knowing what would happen to him, he wrote to the church at Philippi, "I want you to know, brothers and sisters, that what has happened to me has actually served to advance the gospel."[8]

As believers we are both known by our joy and to make God known to others by our joy.

○ ○ ○

I want you to know, looking through the lens of joy is not easy for me. I see darkness just as readily as I do light. So why do I fight to keep my eye on the light?

Poet Christian Wiman wrote,

> Joy is the only inoculation against the despair to which any sane person is prone, the only antidote to the nihilism that wafts through our intellectual atmosphere like sarin gas. More than that: joy is what keeps reality from being sufficient unto itself, which is to say, it is what keeps reality real.[9]

This is why I fight to see goodness and beauty and truth, to keep "reality real." I know how dark it can be out there. You do too. This is why searching for, finding, and sharing joy is energizing, contagious. And why choosing joy in the midst of despair is an act of rebellion.

I'll stand firm in this revolution of joy.

3

in the drive-through car wash

For the times I line up the wheels of my car into the tracks that lead into the car wash tunnel without the guidance of an attendant.[1] The thrill is akin to parallel parking with just an inch on either side, on the first try. I feel like I'm a pilot or an astronaut, and if I do nothing else good that day, You will remind me, that night, as I lay my head down on my pillow, how I rocked the car wash tracks.

For those first jets of soap, sudsy joy, spitting along the sides of my car. That small bit of panic as soap covers each window, like a snowstorm. I am filled with anxious exhilaration as I can't see anything, and then filled with thanks for the glorious streams of clean water that clear away the darkness.

For the big rollers that buff and shine and sheen and burnish and hug and cuddle and bump and embrace.

For the dryer that propels beads of water across my

windshield in a way that can only be described as the way stars would look from the cockpit of the Millennium Falcon when I hit light speed. I throw my body back against my seat and pretend I'm a smuggler, zipping through the galaxies.

For the green light signaling that I may press my foot back on the brake, place the car in drive, and join the regular world once again, clean, exhilarated, fresh, and jubilant.

May I always remember the glimpse of my sons in the rearview mirror that first time I took them through the car wash. They were but toddlers, and the older clasped his hands by his face in delight, and the younger stretched his out as if he was on a raucous rollercoaster. They have never been to an amusement park, but they were just as happy. In their delight, I saw how cynical and careless I'd become, that I could no longer be thrilled by the tunnel of foam.

May they always be the kind of people who find enchantment in taking a spin through Lather Lane. May they never lose the sense of wonder nor let contempt fill them to the point that they cannot be entertained by a $7.99 wash and dry.

4

in capybaras

I have an inexplicable fear of capybaras.

Capybaras are the world's largest rodent. They can grow to be the size of a Saint Bernard.

I mean, a capybara is a real-life R.O.U.S., a "rodent of unusual size" from the film *The Princess Bride*—sans the long tail, sharp teeth, and aggressive manner. Although capybaras can grow up to 150 pounds, these rodents are docile, like, very chill, as if Cheech and Chong and "The Dude" from *The Big Lebowski* had offspring. They are more akin to large guinea pigs than to rats, more interested in just sitting there looking cute than in making any sudden moves. And they live in South America, which is extremely far from where I live in Seattle.

As I said, my fear is unnatural. I have nearly no chance of seeing one picking out fresh flowers at Pike Place Market or riding up the elevator of the Space Needle.

But they freak me the heck out.

Before my husband and I were married, I attended a

seminary in the Northwest where I received a master's degree in intercultural ministry. I wanted to work in the inner city of Los Angeles, and after graduation, I did, ministering to and learning from homeless youth and women and working at soup kitchens, shelters, and after-school programs.

Most of my classmates went on to become missionaries in faraway countries. One dear friend, Kelli, and her husband served as missionaries deep in the jungles of Peru. When I wrote her a letter, it would take weeks to arrive. When my measly jots of a letter finally made it to her hands, it was because a pilot of a nearly pocket-size airplane brought it to her. The pilot would land on the short runway Kelli and her husband had *cut by hand* through the tangle of jungle with a machete so supplies could be delivered. I wrote her stupid things about my life, happy hour banter that did not warrant the heroic journey my insipid letter traveled.

One night just after I drifted off to sleep, I woke sharply, sat up wide-eyed in bed, and asked my husband, who also had just fallen asleep, "Do you think Kelli has seen a capybara?"

My husband, jolted out of his sleep, answered, bleary but kind, "Yeah, probably."

It took me a long time to fall asleep that night while obsessing over this newly discovered information. Did capybaras freak Kelli the heck out too? Did they sit in the path, impeding her way, looking like a roof rat on steroids as she hunted for roots or whatever she did out there in the jungle just trying to survive?

The next day, I wrote Kelli asking if she had ever seen a capybara. It was nearly a month before I received a response:

"Funny you should ask about capybaras. Last night my husband shot one with his bow and arrow. I made capybara hamburgers for dinner. Tastes like pork." She wrote this matter-of-factly. I could hear her voice as I read it. She was rolling her eyes on the other side of the equator, saying things like, "Girl, there are so many *real* dangers out here. A freaking capybara is not one of them."

I must have made an impression because Kelli thought of me on her biyearly trek to the big city of Lima. She was thrilled to go to a restaurant that served Coke with ice, a luxury she hadn't had in months, but she also used the time to purchase a large postcard with one of my furry foes on the front. I shuddered when I pulled it out of the mailbox. I seemed to hear its two front teeth smacking together like an old man with dentures too large for his mouth.

Kelli became one of the members of a small group of friends who liked to make fun of my unfounded fear. They became determined to rid me of this groundless terror.

Their favorite tactic was exposure therapy—basically, subjecting me to as much capybara material as possible. These "friends" sent me links to videos declaring capybaras "the most friendly animals in the world!" The videos featured capybaras nuzzling with sheep dogs, capybaras getting their tummies scratched by a human, and a capybara chillin' in the water with a bird sitting atop its head. I was not amused.

"Face your fear," the friends said as they texted me pictures of capybaras at the San Diego Zoo, which, by the way, is much closer to where I live than South America. And when I found out I was pregnant, my friend Sarah sent the gift of a capybara stuffed animal to the baby shower. I was going to "break the cycle," she said. This child would have his own unfounded fears but not mine.

This bombardment of exposure therapy was annoying for the first twelve years, but now I see how much these friends love me. How they truly want me to be bold, to face my fears, to break the cycle.

And so I sat with the capybara for a little while—not literally, but you know, figuratively, on YouTube. I had access to thousands of videos to watch on my little phone screen in the dark. And I started to see that God has a sense of humor. It's as if, like in some sort of cartoon, he grabbed a rat, made it float in the air, pulled at it to make it larger, then squished it like Play-Doh to make it squatty, and snipped off its tail—the capybara didn't need that anyway; it would only get in the way. Then, before he sat it back down on the ground, he blew a breath of peace upon its hairy back. It would not be like its cousin and scurry and scamper about. This creature would be unruffled, unflappable. It would live in large groups of up to one hundred.

You know how a group of crows is called a murder? A group of capybaras is called a herd, but some have suggested a more clever moniker—a meditation. Yep, a meditation, like a group of Buddhist monks, because they are so Zen. When the world gets to be too much for the monkeys and birds of this world, they can seek out a capybara, just to be around them, to feel their vibe, man.

The capybara's unflappable nature made me think of people in my own life whom I can look to for a sense of tranquility and stability. People who just sit and be. I can freak out like a wiry tamarin, swinging from the ceiling and rattling cages, but those people are calm and stoic.

Several people in my life are like this, but it is my husband who fills this role every day. He watches as I swing and rattle and freak out. He smiles tenderly and reminds me that I shouldn't obsess about something five thousand miles away or even outside our home. For right here, I am loved and safe.

This is when I know God has a sense of humor. He even uses that which I fear to show me I am loved.

5

in puppy bodies

Because their bodies are growing at warp speed, my middle school–aged sons knock picture frames off the walls as they walk by. It is much like when one gets a new car and needs to learn how to parallel park all over again. These boys do not know the dimensions of the new bodies they now find themselves inhabiting.

Because they are children who have taken residence in man-size bodies, they run *every single time* they ascend the stairs of our one-hundred-year-old house. From below, it sounds as the Blitz must have to Londoners in the Underground. My husband hollers up the stairs, "You're too big and too happy to run up the stairs like that." And we all laugh. We laugh because there is a joy in being blissfully unaware of the size of you.

Their bedrooms have holes in the walls, indentations in the drywall from knees and elbows that spasmed in sleep, joints now cut in sharper angles.

There are days when I hear them playing in their rooms

and wonder if they will break through our thin walls like the Kool-Aid Man from the old commercials.

I thought perhaps only they held this awkward liminal space, until one of their friends came over to play Legos. They sat on the floor. Legs flowed into each other, then out the door of the bedroom. In delight, the friend, now round with girth in his morphing body, leaned back on the bed and mistakenly pushed the bed back a foot—into the lath and plaster walls. The boys were stunned at the gaping hole left behind. When the friend showed me the damage, he looked as if he might cry. I told him not to worry. I understood he was like a puppy that had tripped over his own too-big paws.

And because these boys are still but pups, they do not yet know how to hide their emotions—in glee or in sorrow. When they find themselves wounded in body or in spirit, they come to me as they did when they were toddlers. They want to sit on my lap, their legs splayed past mine. We shift and shuffle to find a place where they still fit, where they can still find comfort. And I know, just as their bodies can no longer interlock like puzzle pieces with mine, there will soon be a time when I won't be the one to soothe their soul.

Each month brings a new inch marked on the doorframe where we have marked their growth since preschool. Stray hairs form on their chins and cheeks and upper lips, and my oldest has discovered he can no longer sing along to the Bee Gees "Stayin' Alive." In flashes I get a glimpse of what kind of men they will be, still tender and loving but also strong and protective. During dinner prep I find myself asking if they can reach the pasta sauce on the top shelf of the pantry and then comically requesting them to open the jar when I cannot.

But this morning they arrive, not quite awake, fuzzy and bleary, their eyes not quite open, and fold themselves into my lap. They are still warm and squishy from sleep, and we are awkwardly pressed together between their knobby knees and bony elbows, and I know we will always belong to each other.

6

joy upon hearing "the doors are closing"

Prepare your body, mind, and spirit to be confined to a nineteen-by-twenty-nine-inch space for the next eleven hours. No, you are not condemned to solitary confinement or some type of medieval torture device. You are about to embark on an international flight.

Of course, you feel like a brat for complaining, because a colorful adventure awaits you on the other side. But airline travel takes you to a place where time no longer exists. Where you might not exist. Truly you aren't sure anymore, as you have stood through lines upon lines of utter meaninglessness.

You listen for your boarding group to be called. Did they already call your group? What is your group? Are you standard? Comfort? Plus? Business? Well, we all know you aren't riding first class in those shoes—the ones you wore because they were easy to slip off for security, the ones you can easily slide off later when your feet swell like Ball Park Franks.

But why do you want to board the plane now? So you can sit? For eleven hours?

When your group is finally called to board, you find your seat. It's an aisle seat, just like you booked. You place your carry-on into the overhead compartment, pull your book and your water out of your purse before sliding it under the seat in front of you. You will not buckle your seat belt yet. You will not slip off your shoes. For, any minute, the passenger in the seat next to you will arrive.

You will need to stand up and step into the aisle so they can get comfy. You will smile. You will be pleasant. *But not too pleasant.* You want to make it clear there is a boundary here—you will not entertain any conversation during the next eleven hours. They may kindly tap you on the shoulder should they need to use the lavatory, and you will smile and say, "Of course." But you will not talk about your trip or your children or your work or your latest *story of woe.*

You will eat your dinner. You will have a gin and tonic. You will put on an eye mask. You will go to sleep.

But wait. What's this? They are announcing that the doors are closing!

Everyone appears to be in their seats. No one is coming down the aisle.

Could it be true? Do you really have an empty seat next to you on an international flight?

You do! You do!

Kick off your shoes and celebrate. Of course, you will place your feet on top of said shoes. Spread out, baby! The arm rest is coming up. You don't need no stinkin' arm rest. This is a love seat! You can cross and uncross your legs. Later you might even sit crisscross applesauce right in the middle of the two seats. Think of that. At mealtime, one tray table will be for your food and one for your book.

Look at this. You have *two* pillows and blankets. And two pairs of headphones. You have no idea why you would need two, but you have them. You might actually *sleep* on this flight. You don't have to worry that you might lean on the person next to you when you fall asleep. Or that you might snore in their face or have your mouth wide open (you will).

Is this how people in first class feel? Don't answer that question. You are like Elon Musk or that guy in Mexico with the museum. You're rich! *Rich!* They have their own planes, you say? Shh, quiet, you are ruining this moment. You're *rich*!

7

# of wandering

I'm unsure how it all happened, how I found myself standing in the middle of a public path cut through farmland in the middle of Surrey, England, with one foot stuck in a slop of mud and the other balanced in midair, sans shoe, which was also stuck in the mud. As I stood there in some sort of awkward yoga pose, I couldn't help but laugh, aloud, vociferously until tears streamed down my face because I realized this might be one of the happiest moments of my life.

Six weeks earlier, I was curled up in front of the Christmas tree with my husband. I was spent and tired. I needed inspiration and renewal. I can't remember who said, "Maybe a month in England would be a good idea." It doesn't sound like something either of us would say. But somehow, a month later, I was on a solo trip. No kids. No husband. One overstuffed backpack and not enough warm socks.

With travel points, I was able to book a flight for free, and I stayed with religious communities throughout South

England. I wanted to make this trip as inexpensive as possible. Somehow I landed on a routine of spending my time in church, writing, and walking.

I've been to England before. Each time, I feel God's presence strongly. Is it because I am alone or visiting churches and cathedrals? Or maybe being there connects me to my British ancestors. If I truly search my heart as to why I sense God's presence most in this place, it is because when I go to England, I do not have a to-do list or a schedule; I merely wander. And in this case, I had the luxury of a full month of wandering.

I wasn't in England to be a tourist. I stayed in Benedictine monasteries out in the countryside far from shops and sights. After a morning of writing and prayer, there wasn't much to do. So immediately after lunch, I set out for a long, long walk. It was the middle of winter and began to get dark around 4:00 p.m. I set my phone alarm for 2:15 p.m. to turn back to the monastery guesthouse, lest I get stuck out on streetlight-less roads.

I picked a direction and then wandered.

"What do you want to show me today?" I said aloud as I zipped up my heavy coat.

Walking is much like breathing—footsteps and heartbeat in rhythm together. It becomes automatic, especially when there aren't many fixed points in front of you. You are just going to walk. Meander. For hours. There is no point in hurrying. You will get there. Wherever *there* is.

On those paths, everything became so simple. The tape that played in my head for years—over and over, noise and static, about politics and relationships, old hurts and future worries—just stopped. I could be present, completely present in the moment.

At first, I thought only of walking, my feet moving forward, the impact of the pavement moving through my body. I strayed from the paved road to a dirt path along pastureland where three ponies grazed. They wore plaid blankets, and I could see that though their water trough had frozen in the night, their owner broke through the ice so the ponies could drink. I spoke to them as I walked by, whispering that they were pretty little ponies and that I loved them so much. This seems odd now. Why would I tell these animals that I did not know and that couldn't understand me that I loved them? All I can say is that my inner dialogue was changing. The Psalms, which I was spending hours a day praying with the monks, were becoming part of my inner cadence.

Call it magic or mystery, but the words of the liturgy I heard several times a day placed me in some sort of liminal space—a space between this world and the one we can't usually see. I was existing in a way I had never experienced before.

Not only that, my inner cadence was becoming my outer cadence. I had less internal dialogue. I said things aloud without thinking, to animals, to trees, to God. Everything became prayer. The Scripture was making God's presence evident to me. The Word was made present.

> In you, Lord, I have taken refuge;
> Let me never be put to shame.[1]

Or

I wait for the Lord
more than watchmen wait for the morning.[2]

As I continued along the dirt path, the dark earth cracked with ice even though it had not rained in days. In ravines and ruts, where the last rain had pooled, sheets of ice were left shard, like broken mirrors strewn across the landscape. The wooded path was unkempt. Probably only cut back in the summer. I brushed branches out of the way and traipsed through undergrowth. I was walking without a destination or reason. A full month of this, day in and day out.

What am I doing? I'm walking and praying for days while my family is at home working, going to school, making meals, and washing dishes. Am I a self-indulgent brat?

Sixteenth-century writer and father of the essay, Michel de Montaigne, understood the tension I was experiencing. Being alone just for the sake of being alone is one thing, but seeking "solitude for devotion's sake, filling [one's] minds with the certainty of God's promises for the life to come, is much more sane and appropriate." Well, thank you Michel. I am not crazy or selfish. He wrote on, "Their objective is God, infinite in goodness and power: the soul can find there matters to slake her desires in perfect freedom."[3] Yes, this is what I want: to understand God's goodness, to see his power, and to grow in freedom.

Before I left for this trip, I sent a message to my favorite seminary professor. I told him my plan for England. He replied, "Being alone with the Lord is truly one of life's great blessings."

His words returned to my mind as I berated myself for the luxury of being able to walk and pray for days.

Isn't this what life is all about? Being with God? Knowing him? Shouldn't I spend my entire life looking for opportunities like this?

The path turned and opened as I found myself on the top of a hill with farmland spread out before me. It was brisk, and now without trees to shield me from the sun, it was bright enough to pull out my sunglasses. Sheep dotted the landscape, as did cottages made of sandstone. The air smelled clean and woodsy.

This is what awe feels like.

No, this is what love feels like.

I knew, right there on the top of that English hill, that God was with me, showing me a sight he knew I'd be dazzled by, just as I would if I were with one of my sons, showing them something they would be delighted by.

I was discovering on those long prayerful walks how much love is entwined with joy. How knowing I am loved, believing I am loved, opens me up to joy. This was fortifying.

I'd been in this space before.

What seems like a lifetime ago, devastated from a broken marriage engagement, I moved to Portland, Oregon, where I knew no one. All week I worked a dead-end job, and on the weekends, without friends or money, I took long hikes in the Columbia River Gorge. I was sad and angry. I'd had big plans for my life, and now they were gone. I had invested six years of my life planning on that life, focusing on that man, and quite simply, ignoring God.

The lush green trails of the gorge were splashed with waterfalls, and every branch, dripped with moss and lichen, looked like something out of a Dr. Seuss book. It was all very different from the dry, treeless landscape of Los Angeles where I grew up. Lonely, I explored new trails each weekend until my loneliness turned into enchantment and the volume of my internal dialogue was deafening—and I realized, I was praying. Not only was I praying, but I knew God was listening. It was as if he were standing right next to me in front of a fairy-tale waterfall with tears in his eyes as I whined, no, *lamented,* over my derailed plans. But that life was not what he had planned. And I knew I could do better. He had much more planned for me.

That day in Oregon was like the day in England. I discovered I was loved. Knew I was loved. And I learned I needed to trust God to discover what was next.

I want to tell you how difficult my return home from England was—family injury, betrayal, loss of work and community, distortion of truth. But that's a story for another time. What you need to know is that what I learned wandering those paths in England sustained me during those difficult months. I was fortified. Fearless.

On those paths walking with God, I was discovering who I was becoming, who God created me to be, my place in this world, and who God truly is.

When my phone alarm chimed telling me it was time to turn back to the monastery, I decided to make a loop instead of covering the same ground. Thirty minutes in, I looked across a flat, open field with a fenced path cut through. I could see a dozen or so villagers across the valley, perhaps half a mile away, walking toward me, in pairs and solo.

The path long and clear, I could now see what lay ahead

for the first time that afternoon. I wanted to run and sing, like I was in *The Sound of Music*, for the triumphant view of luxurious farmland and open skies. I quickened my gait to a near skip, and that's when I looked closer and realized that the entire pathway, for half a mile, was mud. Thick, wet, soddened earth. The word one might use if one were biblical or British is *mire*.

If I turned around, I would not make it back to the monastery by sunset.

The only way was through.

And that is when I was grateful for the fence that lined the path. I held on to it like a toddler learning to walk, inching my way through. Bramble, now dried in the winter, had grown through the fence. I searched for brushwood without thorns that I could break off and use for a makeshift cane.

Villagers grew closer to me on the path. I could now see that they were not wearing Ecco walking shoes like me, but every single one of them wore knee-high wellies and walked easily through the muck. Thank God for that "Keep Calm and Carry On" spirit; none of them laughed at me.

I imagined them talking to each other over a pint later that night.

Did you see that American walking around with the big tan coat?

Yes, I ran into her yesterday coming back from East Shalford.

She doesn't seem to have a clue where she's going, but she's happy enough to get there.

Yeah, I think she might be simple.

"Afternoon," I said, nodding my head to two women in puffer coats and knit caps.

"Afternoon," they responded in unison, stoic, reserved.

I put one foot in front of the other. My cadence was no longer rhythmic but a *squealch* and *squirch* arrhythmia. I could do this. "I may be a city girl, but I'm from hearty stock just the same as them," I thought.

Until I got stuck.

I looked down at my shoe stuck in the mud and contemplated pretending I was in some sort of modified tree pose, when I suddenly couldn't believe the utter ridiculousness of it all and began to laugh. Losing my balance, I clung to the fence, doubling over in hysterical glee.

An old man in a flat cap and boots his own grandfather might have given him whistled for his herding dog trailing behind.

"I think you've ruined your trainers there."

"I think you're right!" I didn't care. It was glorious.

Mustering up my best Churchill impression, I added, "The only way is through!"

8

in a smile

When my son was a toddler, he smiled and said hello to every single person he passed. It wasn't a curt howdy. It was one of those smiles, big and bright, where his eyes turned into little half-moons and his entire face transformed into light itself. He sang the greeting long and harmoniously, *Hellllooo,* as if he'd been longing to see you, he had missed you, and he wasn't sure he'd ever see you again in this lifetime.

This greeting was aimed at friends and strangers alike.

Shoppers at Costco were taken aback. So were the homeless who sat in doorways of downtown Seattle. Or neighbors on our walks after lunch who had lived next door for years but had never returned my hellos or even looked up when I passed before I had children.

Coming from a toddler, the smile was disarming. I could see it change people. They warmed—first to him, then to me.

I remember a nine-year-old boy saying, "It's like he's looking right into my soul." And once, in my car at a stoplight, my son's smile softened a homeless man, standing with a sign, into a pool of tears. I rolled down my window to hand him a mandarin orange I had in my purse. "You've got a sweet one there," he said, wiping the tears from his eyes. He'd been seen.

There is power in recognition, in acknowledging the existence of another human. Even if it is for a brief instant. In that moment, we are connected. We are not alone.

Maybe my son picked up this proclivity from me, or perhaps I from him, but either way, I've been smiling more. I smile at the grocery store, at the library, on my errands around my city of Seattle. There are noticeable results.

For one, I feel a little foolish, especially living in a place like I do, where people do not smile much and take themselves way too seriously. Sometimes I wonder if they even like other people. But then, isn't that every place?

Many look at me strangely, as if I am mad. Not angry, but like I have escaped from an asylum somewhere. Or like I am on drugs. But then, everyone is on drugs in Seattle. Just not the type that make you smile.

So I stop smiling. And then I feel rotten inside. I feel like I am hiding something. Because I am.

In Scripture, when Moses returns from Mount Sinai with two tablets of the law, he does not realize his *face is glowing*.[1]

This was actually the second set of tablets. The first set Moses famously broke when he saw the Israelites worshiping a golden calf on his return. It is after Israel's unfaithfulness that God gives Moses a glimpse of his glory. Moses sees God's back, and his face becomes radiant. The Israelites are afraid to come near Moses. As a solution, he wears a veil over his face. Scripture doesn't say whether Moses decides to do this or if the people ask him to, but he does.

When I was a kid, I wondered if his face still shone through the veil, like how, as a child, I'd put my hand over a flashlight and the light would shine through my skin. Did that happen to Moses?

But the biggest thing that bothered me then, and still bothers me now, is why the Israelites were afraid. Why didn't they want to see Moses's radiant face—the face reflecting the glory of God? Was the light too bright a contrast against the darkness of their sin? Were they ashamed?

So I smile again and say hello as I pass people on the street. I don't care if people think I am simple or a fool. I want them to know there is another way. We do not have to live in isolation or avoid eye contact. We do not need to hide from each other. We can connect.

I know that sounds like delusions of grandeur. I promise you, I know I am not Moses. And I know that a smile isn't going to change the world. But that smile, that hello, reflects what has happened in my heart. I have been transformed by God's love. His love is living and breathing within me. And I want to acknowledge and honor the *imago Dei*, or image of God, within others—even if only for a second.

Many church traditions have rituals one performs when interacting with the holy: bowing, kneeling, lifting hands, making the sign of the cross. These are outward signs, a visible expression of what has happened, is happening, on a spiritual level: that you have experienced God's grace in your life. A smile and greeting are another example of this. In this act, you are acknowledging the image of God imprinted on the person before you. And in doing so, you become a channel for God's grace.

These smiling encounters still vary. Some think I may be unhinged. "Do I know you?" some ask. Or "Are you someone famous?" That one makes me laugh. Many are wary. I understand. They wonder if I want something from them or whether perhaps I'm selling something. Nope. A smile is just a gift. It's not much, but it's free. It costs nothing to give, and I want nothing in return.

I have noticed a small change, especially in places I frequent. Many now smile and say hello to me first. We've begun to learn each other's names. Our interest and openness spreads to others around us, contagious, until it becomes the ethos of the coffee shop, the gym, the grocery store. Smiling is contagious. This smile is changing the culture around me. In responding to Christ's love, I feel it changing me too. I feel more connected to its source. I feel connected to other people.

And yet I do notice that there are some for whom a smile is painful. I see it in my daily interactions, as if my smile and kindness burn. Perhaps these people have been hurt. They do not trust kindness. I remember feeling that way. I wondered how genuine the kindness was. Would it require something of me? Was it shallow? Untrue?

I am reminded that it was God's kindness that drew me to him.[2] It was kindness that welcomed me. In his kindness, he invited me to receive his love. And for those who are unsure, he does not withdraw; he does not withhold his gestures—but he is gentle.

And then there are still others, like the Israelites, who can't bear to behold such light. This reminds me of Paul's words to the church at Corinth: "We are to God the pleasing aroma of Christ among those who are being saved and those who are perishing. To the one we are an aroma that brings death; to the other, an aroma that brings life."[3]

Joy is a consequence of knowing God. God is the source of my joy, my smile. He is the light upon my face. I must be bold and let it shine through me. Paul, again, spoke of this to the church at Corinth in his second letter, saying we are not like Moses, covering our faces, but rather, we, "who with unveiled faces contemplate the Lord's glory, are being transformed into his image with ever-increasing glory, which comes from the Lord."[4]

My friend Monica was recently stopped by a stranger on the street asking for directions. After exchanging the needed information, the woman looked closely at Monica and said, "Wow, your skin is glowing! What is your skin care routine?" Monica smiled and said, "That's my faith you're seeing." The woman looked at her closer, softened her eyes, and then widened them. "Oh, yes," she gasped. "I see it now. I see it."

9

in Van Gogh's *Sunflowers*

My back aches and my feet throb from walking through London's National Gallery all morning. I don't mind my crumbling body, for I am content. A museum serves as sacred space for me. It is often quiet, nearly silent, even as droves of people walk through the halls. Museum goers hold their hands behind their backs, careful not to touch, holding reverence for the space around them. In creating, the artist reveals his connection to the Divine, his image reflected within us, igniting us to create. Each room in the museum holds the possibility of finding a window to the transcendent, a view of God's grace and holiness, beauty and love through the eyes of an artist. I saw many of these windows this morning. Caravaggio's *The Supper at Emmaus* captures the moment when Christ reveals himself to grieving disciples through the breaking of bread. In Jan van Eyck's *The Arnolfini Portrait* of a newly married couple with all their fine goods, the mirror at the back of the painting reveals the surprise of the painter himself. My heart is bursting with God's goodness as I bask in such skill.

I know it's time for lunch because my stomach is growling aloud, but I can't bear to move. I've noticed something peculiar. I'd like to stand here for a few more minutes to follow my curiosity.

The museum tells a chronological story. Its hallways and galleries are configured into a timeline of the panorama of art history. Here, in room 43, twenty paintings line the four walls. One can enter the room from either side, but most come from room 42, where the monochromatic shades of brown, gray, and dull green swathe its nineteenth-century landscapes.

Nearly every person who walks into room 43 comes to a full stop when they enter. It's as if their senses are overloaded. They can't walk and see at the same time, for the entire room is aflood with light and color. Moving from those dull earth tones to this near-technicolor room of the Impressionists reminds me of my Grandpa Bravo's refrain, "Now we got color TV!"

There are paintings from Toulouse-Lautrec, Pissarro, and Cézanne, but the same painting seems to call to each person as they enter. I watch as they look around the room, their eyes widen, and their entire countenance changes, and often I even hear an "Awww" as they walk directly to Van Gogh's *Sunflowers*.

If you haven't seen the painting, I feel funny describing it to you; it's a bunch of sunflowers in a vase—and some of them are dying. I know. That doesn't sound spectacular, but trust me, it is. I mean, it has to be, right? To invoke such a strong response from people?

To paraphrase Alice Walker in her poem on Van Gogh, "If There Was Any Justice," Van Gogh would want me to have this painting. This painting radiates. I once heard it said that it looks as if it is backlit, as if light itself is coming through the painting.

In 1888, before his hospital stint, before the infamous ear incident, Van Gogh moved to Arles, France. He rented a beautiful house in town, which he called the Yellow House, for obvious reasons. After years of moving constantly, this was the first time Van Gogh anticipated staying put. This would be not just a house but a home. He organized a studio on the ground floor, and on the second floor was his room, which he famously painted, and a second bedroom that would serve as a guest room. He envisioned inviting artists to visit and stay in that room. Here in this Yellow House, the two artists would create and inspire each other.

So when renowned artist Paul Gauguin accepted his invitation, Van Gogh was elated. He set out to make the guest room as welcoming as possible. He decided to paint two canvases of his favorite flowers, sunflowers. Van Gogh was pleased with the way the paintings turned out. Unable to paint outdoors one windy end-of-summer week, awaiting his friend's arrival, Van Gogh painted two more sunflower paintings in a single week. When Gauguin arrived, he liked the paintings so much, he wanted one, so Van Gogh painted more, seven in total, each slightly different. The paintings have different numbers of flowers, three to fifteen, inside the vase. Four of these paintings have various shades of blue as a background, but three, including the one at the National Gallery, have a yellow background. Yes, yellow flowers against a yellow background. And the vase is also yellow. Van Gogh lightened the shades of yellow by mixing with white, but in the entire painting, only three colors are used: green, the thinnest band of blue, and yellow.

○ ○ ○

As I stand in front of this near-completely yellow masterpiece, it is clear to me what Van Gogh was attempting to paint. It wasn't sunflowers. He wanted to paint joy.

Moving to Arles produced a prolific period in Van Gogh's artwork, one of which is *infused* with yellow. Many imagine that maybe this is because he enjoyed sipping absinthe at the cafés at which he painted during this period. Others blame the digitalis, or foxglove, plant he ingested to dull his epilepsy. Both are known to inflame the subject's perception of the color yellow.[1] For Van Gogh, the color yellow represented sunshine, gratitude, and Christ, the light of the world.

Van Gogh had synesthesia, a condition in which one sensory perception prompts another. For Van Gogh, color invoked sound.[2] He once wrote to his brother, "Some [artists] have a nervous manner that gives their technique something of the singularity of the sound a violin makes."[3] Van Gogh said some artists were reminiscent of a piano, others (like Millet) an organ. Some have also researched how Van Gogh was able to paint the turbulent flow of light as in his masterpiece *The Starry Night*.[4] What if Van Gogh could paint emotion too? What if he could paint joy? What if, just as we feel dizzy or in motion in front of his paintings of turbulent flow, we feel his joy when we are in front of a painting like *Sunflowers*?

At thirty-five, Van Gogh had already lived in over thirty residences when he painted these *Sunflowers*. After years of feeling displaced, he finally had a home. Not only that, after decades of trying out different vocations, including working in a gallery and being a minister, Van Gogh finally felt established in the art world. He was going to create his artist retreat in this home. When I look at *Sunflowers*, I see it as a prayer of thanksgiving for all these things. The overwhelming light of yellow tries to capture and symbolize all this gratitude.

And we know the rest of the story. We know about his mental breakdown, the mutilation of his own ear, how he self-medicated by eating his paints, how he was committed to an asylum for a year, and how he eventually simply couldn't handle the inner turmoil and went into a cornfield and shot himself.

I think that is why we love and connect with this painting so much: We also know joy and despair. To know that someone who felt despair so greatly also felt joy gives us hope. In auspicious anticipation of his friend's arrival, Van Gogh was happy. A man who did not and would not feel joy often, did, in this one magical summer.

We can see the window into the transcendent in this painting of gratitude, for his home, for his friend Gauguin. Van Gogh, a former pastor who struggled with his faith, prayed in the only way he could: a visual prayer of thanksgiving.

At Van Gogh's funeral, a white sheet was draped over

his coffin. His friends brought sunflowers to adorn it. Artist and friend Émile Bernard said yellow was Vincent's "favorite color, the symbol of the light that he dreamed of as being in people's hearts as well as in works of art."[5]

I think somehow we connect with intense love and loss as we stand before the painting, a prayer in hues of medallion, honey, and gold, masquerading as sunflowers. It connects us through time and humanity and joy. We too struggle, have inner turmoil; sometimes we self-medicate. But we see how Van Gogh marked the moment when joy broke through. How will we mark such moments?

10

in laundry

When I was growing up, my family moved nearly every year within the same couple of adjacent cities, renting small bungalows in Southern California. Most did not have the luxury of a washer and dryer. So, a few Saturdays a month, usually while my father was at work, my mother squished my two younger sisters, me, a few rolls of quarters, and several loads of laundry into her seaweed-green Ford Pinto and drove to the laundromat.

I can imagine what a chore this must have been for my mother. She was a teenager when I was born. When I try to place my child self in that fluorescent world of whirling machines and institutional white walls, I am about six, my sister Sara is two-and-a-half, and Bonnie is just a baby of one. My mother must have sweat unloading all of us and all that laundry from the car and into the washers, but I remember nearly cheering when she said we were going to the laundromat.

It was a thrilling challenge to try to find enough washers

in a row. If we had to split up our loads, the challenge then became keeping our eyes on the odd one out. Would we forget about it? Once, we forgot about my favorite blanket, the patchwork one my mother sewed with scraps from my old pajamas. It was lost in the vortex, never to be seen again. From then on, my mother placed the large box of powdered detergent atop the lid of the odd washer to remind us to put that load in the dryer too.

Sometimes we couldn't get all the washers we needed at first and would have to start a few loads, then a few more as other washers freed up. I knew then we would be there for hours.

I didn't mind this. We were the type of family that didn't get out of the house often. We didn't have money to go to the zoo or an amusement park. But the laundromat was great fun. My sisters and I were allowed to walk up and down the aisles, which seemed like a great freedom. Bonnie had just begun to walk, and Sara and I took turns holding her hand and guiding her through what seemed like rows and rows of machines.

Sometimes my sisters climbed into a rolling hamper, and I pushed them about. They held on tight to the sides, their eyes widening with delight, and squealed as I took the corners. For us, it was like a ride at Disneyland. I could do this only if there weren't many other people at the laundromat. My mother didn't want us to annoy the other women—mostly Mexican mothers, some with children just like us, eating burritos that looked scrumptious.

My favorite part of the outing was when my sisters needed to nap. They might curl up on a chair or inside one of the rolling hampers, and I sat and watched the dryers. The sound was hypnotic. Now I know many people enjoy listening to dryer sounds. They might even listen to that rhythmic drumming on loop to help them fall asleep. This explains why my sisters napped so well. I think of them there, warm and cozy near the dryers, the sound rhythmically lulling them to sleep. Perhaps my mother covered them with a towel straight out of the dryer, warm and smelling of fabric sheets. Or maybe I just wished she would have, because that sounds delicious.

While they napped, I watched the laundry tumble through the glass window of the dryer. I'd find one item, perhaps my favorite jammies or my sister's bright pink sock, and watch it rise, then fall, spin, then plummet. As I watched, nothing in the world existed but me and that splash of color. My mind erased into absolute peace.

I wonder now if this was the beginnings of prayer working on me. Repetition. Meditation. Just basking in the light of something that dazzled.

When the dryer timers chimed, my work began. I filled the hampers with heaps of warm clothes, pushed them over to my mother, and we set to the task of folding each item, as there was more space to fold at the laundromat than at our home. Years before KonMari, my mother showed me how to fold each item the correct way. Towels were folded into squares, as that's how they fit in the cabinets at home most easily. Shirts that were not hung were folded into thirds from the sides, then thirds again, top to bottom. She showed me how to use the counters at the laundromat to smooth the material, press it as an iron would, so each piece was fresh and crisp and good.

When we drove home, the sunshine from outside amplified the clean scent inside our car. I am not sure why, but I felt proud. Perhaps it was because what had been soiled and stinky returned home transformed. Our colorful little packages new again. Happy. My mother carried us, then the cheerful baskets back into our home, and we unloaded them into our drawers and closets for a fresh start.

Writer and poet Kathleen Norris wrote about the ritualistic movements of laundry in her marvelous little book *The Quotidian Mysteries: Laundry, Liturgy and "Women's Work."* Yes, times have changed from both Norris's (who is older than I) childhood and my own, but laundry still tends to be "women's work." Even though just as many women are in the workforce as men now, usually it is women who come home to tend to the laundry.

The reason I am the main one to do laundry in my house is because I like it. Sometimes I may not realize it! But I like it. For various reasons, I'd rather be the one to do the laundry.

Maybe I like doing the laundry because although it is never-ending, there is a sense of accomplishment in completing a load from start to finish. As Norris puts it, "There are days when it seems a miracle to be able to make dirty things clean."[1] Some days none of my projects have found resolution. Miscommunication still lingers out there with a friend or family member. My gas tank on the car is nearly empty. I don't get to the last five things on my to-do list. But at the end of the day, I sit down to fold all the laundry that I moved between the washer and dryer throughout the day. Before each family member goes to bed, they grab their stack of clean clothes and put them in their drawers. And at night when I lay my head on my pillow and go over the day, I think, "Well, at least I got three loads of laundry done."

In Alice McDermott's gorgeous novel *The Ninth Hour*, Sister Illuminata knows her work in the convent's basement laundry is her vocation. With "scared solemnity"[2] she shows her assistant how to tend to each item that comes in from the poor box or from the homes of the sick. When Sister Illuminata sees sheets soiled with "mucus tinged with blood,"[3] she knows there has been a birth and makes a sign of the cross, praying for both mother and child. Perhaps this is why it is "woman's work," for laundry spills secrets of love and loss, of sickness and pain.

Norris writes that many of our "laundry rituals" are "inherited from a mother or grandmother."[4] Maybe we like this connection to the women before us. We miss these women and keep present in the daily tasks that connected us to them. Yes, I still fold my towels as my mother showed me, and if I close my eyes, I can watch my grandmother iron my button-down shirt for church on Sunday morning: the way she always started on the collar, sprayed water on the sleeves, and ironed strong creases on the arms. I use a cold-water rinse for nearly everything because that is what my mother taught me, and I now wonder if her mother taught her the same thing.

Maybe you too like doing laundry because you have a story similar to mine. You too have a story of doing laundry with women in your family. Maybe you shared stories while you worked or learned something new, like the trick to get out a grass or blood stain, or simply enjoyed being together. You were accomplishing something, together. These women are made present in this small act. We have a glimpse of their presence once again and are connected to the eternal in the mundane.

Like my pink-sock-in-the-dryer prayer, Norris noticed that God's "presence is revealed even in the meaningless workings of daily life."[5] Is it because we can do many of these tasks on autopilot? Our mind quiets and we can hear him speak softly. Norris points out that what might seem like a "ludicrous attention to detail in the book of Leviticus, involving God in the minutiae of daily life—all the cooking and cleaning of a people's domestic life—might be revisioned as the very love of God. A God who cares so much as to desire to be present to us and everything we do."[6]

When I look at it this way, I realize that the peace I felt when I watched the pink sock in the dryer and everything else around me vanished did feel a lot like love.

I know I'm going to sound silly, but this makes me teary with gratitude. I don't go to church every day. There may be days when I do not pray. But every day, I must do laundry, wash dishes, make a bed, and perhaps push a vacuum around. God loves me enough to be present in that? *I* don't even want to be present in that.

And again, at the risk of sounding simple, isn't this a bit of the incarnation? Not only did God become man, flesh, and Saint Paul says our bodies connected to him, but in making our bodies a temple for his Spirit, he also gives us opportunity to make the work of our hands holy. He was there as my mother and I smoothed our shirts against the white counter of the laundromat. He is there as I end the day folding my sons' clothes into colorful little packages for them to carry up to their rooms.

In the Gospels, Jesus quotes a beautiful Scripture from the book of Deuteronomy: "Love the LORD your God with all your heart and with all your soul and with all your strength."[7] It goes on to say that the Word of the Lord should always be on our hearts. We should "impress" it on our children. We should talk about Scripture when we "sit at home and when [we] walk along the road, when [we] lie down and when [we] get up."[8] This is why on the doorframe of Jewish households you will see a *mezuzah*, words from the Torah in a small decorative case, usually the size of a tube of lip balm. Some Jews even tie little boxes containing Scripture to their hands or foreheads, as it says in the next verses, so his Word is literally always before them. Reminders like these invite God into each moment of our lives. Not just going to church but also getting dressed for the day, grabbing our car keys before leaving the house, and even doing laundry can be prayer, little acts of love between us and The One Who Always Existed.

Norris says that many women wrote her about their own laundry stories after her essay on laundry appeared in *The New York Times Magazine*. One of her favorite responses came from an Israeli woman who wrote that during the Gulf War "the government had warned people not to hang clothes out of doors, as a gas attack would pollute them. The mother of an infant, she had defied the warnings and hung her baby's clothes out of doors as a visible sign of hope."[9]

McDermott uses her character Sister Illuminata to illuminate this same sentiment, as she hung the nuns' clean clothes out in the courtyard sun: "A clean cloth—Immaculate and pure—to place against mankind's wounds. She had felt, the fragrant steam rising, the joy of it, the rightness of it. No help in putting a soiled, sullied thing to what was itself based and infected."[10] The clothes of these religious women were a symbol of their prayers and their work in the world. Their clothes too were a sign of hope.

This is true for even us, out of war, out of religious life. My friend Nicole, a mother of twelve, tells me she doesn't mind doing the laundry for her large family. At the end of each load, beauty is restored, hope realized. Redemption.

11

joyful Mary and Christ

My friend Marina Gross-Hoy created an amusing video clip for her Instagram account called "Tired Moms at the Met."[1] The reel pans over works of art in which the mother is portrayed as incredibly spent and overwhelmingly exhausted as she holds her child. It moves through artworks, both paintings and sculptures, that span centuries from Byzantine, Mannerism, and Baroque periods. Images show vacant, disconnected eyes, or eyes that seem to say, "Get me out of here," as the child nurses at the mother's breast. All these flowing images are set to Louis Armstrong's lackadaisical rendition of "La Vie En Rose." The result is hilarious.

Mothers overwhelmingly connected with the reel, saying things like, "Yep, this is what I look like 90 percent of the time," or "Even artists can't ignore the reality of motherhood." At last count, the video had been viewed nearly four million times. Friends and family members tagged each other, saying, "This is so us."

I find this connection between art and motherhood especially thrilling because these artworks portray Mary and the Christ child. Religious and nonreligious women alike were connecting with Mary in a new way. One commenter wrote, "It's a lot of pressure to raise our Lord and Savior Jesus Christ," and another, "If you birthed Jesus and are still tired . . . the rest of us are doooomed!"

As grueling as motherhood is, there are moments of such indescribable delight that most mothers forget the pain of childbirth and would gladly do it all over again just because of the way their children sink into their neck when they are picked up or laugh when the garbage disposal is flipped on.

And then I wonder, Did Mary delight in Jesus in this way?

Did Jesus do cute things that made his mother laugh? Of course he did.

○ ○ ○

During my month-long solo trip to England, I arrived at the London Jesuit Centre exhausted and disoriented after a red-eye flight for my first leg of the journey. When I travel alone, I often stay at religious organizations that offer guest rooms. They are safe and inexpensive, and I can stay close to the rhythms of prayer while a guest. The Jesuit Centre is located right next to Farm Street Church in the middle of Mayfair, London. I knew I could attend daily Mass while visiting.

The attendant at the desk gave me a key card and pointed

me up the Victorian iron-and-wood-railed stairs to find my room. Incredibly high ceilings echoed each footstep up to the third floor. The Centre had recently been remodeled, and this Victorian-era architecture was paired with modern glass doors, opened with electronic key cards between secured hallways. As I walked through the hallway to the guest rooms, lights at foot level automatically lit my path, like the *Starship Enterprise*. Then I saw them.

At the end of the hall of guest rooms was a fifteenth-century Italian sculpture of Mary holding the Christ child. And they were smiling! I nearly ran toward them to get a better look. Mary looked incredibly majestic in royal clothes. The stone had once been painted vibrant colors, now faded through the years. There were indentations where precious jewels once lay. Christ looked to be about two years old. Mary held him with one hand on her hip as many mothers do. Toddler Christ held a bird, perhaps a toy, but perhaps a real bird, as it appeared to be biting his thumb. Christ appeared playful, happy. I don't mean to state the obvious, but he looked like a child. Not a pious, otherworldly being, akin to an alien appearing under a light in *The X-Files*, but a real kid. You know, like we once were.

And Mary did not look (and I do not mean this disrespectfully) like a hot mess, as in that "Tired Mothers at the Met" reel. She was regal, put together. She looks comfortable in herself and with her child. In fact, she is wearing *poulaines*, the pointed-toe shoes that fashionable women of the fifteenth century wore.

Now, I understand that Mary and Jesus were not wealthy. But they are often portrayed as such in art. I think what artists are trying to convey in this portrayal is our esteem for them, that they are above all other men and women.

But what I think this anonymous fifteenth-century artist was able to depict was Mary's confidence. She knew who she was and whom she belonged to. And she knew her vocation, a job she was born to do and would do well.

After spending a good amount of time with the sculpture, I remembered I needed to find my room. I turned to look and found it was the one closest to the sculpture. For this leg of the journey, this joyful Mary and Christ would watch over my sleep. I thought of the refrain throughout Scripture, "The LORD will watch over your coming and going."[2] That next week, I would stop before them for a prayer when I left my room for Mass or a walk or to find food. I couldn't shake that little bird in Jesus's hand from my mind. It reminded me of his words in the gospel of Matthew: "Look at the birds of the air; they do not sow or reap or store away in barns, and yet your heavenly Father feeds them. Are you not much more valuable than they?"[3] I knew he cares about me too. And I began to connect with Mary in a new way—understanding that she was a very good mother—and I am too.

○ ○ ○

I was hesitant to have children. My parents weren't the best models. They were neglectful, inattentive, and frankly, abusive. I spent much of my childhood fending for myself and taking care of my younger sisters. I did not want to do that again.

My husband saw things in me that I couldn't. He could

see I would be a wonderful mother. It is a strange thing to say aloud. In motherhood circles, we are supposed to downplay our successes. But I know I am a good mother. Despite my models and with my husband's and God's love, I have found my way. My sons know they are loved, and I have given them a good balance of support and kicking them in the butt to get out there and try on their own.

And here is the thing I never would have known about motherhood: just how much I delight in my children.

My youngest was a humongous baby. Despite, or perhaps because, he was only breast-fed for the first nine months of his life, he was roly-poly, with folds upon folds of fat, the kind in which things get lost. And because we are of a culture that likes to point out the obvious as a term of endearment, even if it is negative, my Mexican family would out-and-out call him Chubbus.

Once we had guests visiting who were not of our ethnic background. When my baby woke from his afternoon nap, I brought him out to meet my friends, and my oldest, who was only two at the time and could barely talk, said as clear as a bell, "Chubbus! You're awake!"

My friends were polite and pretended not to understand what my toddler had said but also asked again what the baby's name was. I couldn't stop snort-laughing, and then they knew it was okay to laugh. Even though, at just thirteen years old, my youngest son is now six feet, three and a half inches and as skinny as a skeleton on a diet, to this day we all greet him in the morning with "Chubbus! You're awake!"

I think about this with Mary. Were there things Jesus said that would send her into a giggling fit? I mean, he was the very definition of precocious. This is not something I thought about much until I saw that sculpture in London. I grew up in a faith tradition that did not focus on Mary. In fact, to do so was called idolatrous. When I first began attending Catholic Masses, I felt a hesitant tug in my heart whenever she was brought up. But as a woman who did not have a good and loving model in my own mother, I now see how meditating on Mary can heal my wounded mothering heart. Mary was the best mother ever.

When the angel Gabriel visited her as a teenager, offering her the vocation of a lifetime, the epic job of jobs, she didn't flinch. She didn't back down. "I am the Lord's servant. . . . May your word to me be fulfilled."[4]

She ran to the only other person who would understand, her aging cousin Elizabeth, who was also miraculously pregnant, and upon simply hearing Mary's voice, John, the child within Elizabeth, "leaped for joy."[5]

I think we say these words of Scripture without feeling at church. In liturgical settings they are read nearly monotone. But when an unborn child simply heard the voice of Christ's mother, he leaped for joy. Joy inspires joy. A stoic, unaffected person does not invoke a joyous reaction.

And then Mary breaks into song! She begins praising God in a canticle that calls upon the praise of Hannah centuries before her. "My spirit rejoices," she sings, and "from now on all generations will call me blessed."[6] In the Magnificat, Mary knows where she has come from and the magnitude of what she has been called to do. She trusts in the "mighty" power of her God. She stands in joy as defiance in the face of evil, of original sin, crushing the head of the serpent Satan himself.

When her child is born and amazed shepherds come to her bedside to see the baby and tell her all the angels sang to them, announcing his birth, Mary "treasured up all these things and pondered them in her heart."[7] All this singing, yet we portray her as stoic.

My mother-in-law told me that she can't glance over at a partition in her kitchen without seeing my husband at three or four years old peeking over it at her. He is now nearly fifty years old. Wouldn't Mary have stories and connections to Jesus in such a way as this? Do we think Jesus and Mary changed the world with resignation? Indifference? Did he not run and squeal as a child? Did she not run after him, scoop him up in her arms with a tickle and a kiss? Did she not marvel at how beautiful this child was becoming?

Now as young teens, my sons are changing as quickly as they did as toddlers. Back then the changes were new words and abilities; now it is ideas and responsibilities. It is a delight to see them sort through the world and its complications in ways I would never have the patience even to attempt. And these boys, now young men, are fun to be with. They have become so interesting that some of our relatives and family friends *want* to hang out with them. They are happy to give the boys a ride to jiujitsu or come over to share a meal or play board games, knowing I am not the type of mother who enjoys board games. These adults enjoy the company of my sons. They find their enthusiasm for life contagious.

I think of this when I ponder what Catholics call the "Joyful Mysteries." These are joyful moments in Mary's life with Christ. There are five: the annunciation, the visitation with Elizabeth, Christ's birth, his presentation in the temple, and Jesus's parents finding him in the temple. It's this last one that throws me for a loop. The holy family had been traveling for the Passover, and somehow on their way home, twelve-year-old Jesus was lost. For three days his parents looked for him. Can you imagine how frantic they must have been? My son walks into a dead zone with no cell coverage on the way home from school, and I freak out. When Joseph and Mary finally found Jesus, he was in the temple, "sitting among the teachers, listening to them and asking them questions."[8]

Mary was wrought with emotion. "Son, why have you treated us like this? Your father and I have been anxiously searching for you." These are some of the few words of Mary we have documented. I appreciate that she is not a pushover. She isn't quietly resigned. Jesus responds, "Didn't you know I had to be in my Father's house?" Scripture says Jesus's parents still didn't understand what he was saying to them. But they returned home together as a family, and Jesus was "obedient to them." Again, Mary "treasured all these things in her heart."

Here is why I think it is a Joyful Mystery. Mary realized she accomplished what she set out to do. She raised a son who could take care of himself, who asked good questions. He was a deep thinker and the type of young man others wanted to be around. Her son had found what he was meant to do.

Mary knew her son well, and now there was joy in seeing others get to know him too. And the joy of seeing the beginning of his vocation unfold.

○ ○ ○

It was difficult to leave the joyful Mary and Christ child sculpture at the Jesuit Centre, but I didn't want to outwear my welcome. On the three-hour train ride west to Devon, and then the hour-long bus trip to my next location, Buckfast Abbey, I thought how it was as if I'd had my own sculpture all week. Mary and Jesus's relationship to each other and then to me became alive in my mind. I knew they would always be with me in some way, but I'd miss them.

I exited the bus with my enormous backpack strapped to my back and walked the long driveway to Buckfast Abbey. I saw the Gothic steeples of the abbey first. They towered out of the mist on that gray January morning. The abbey's history is nearly one thousand years old. Eager to see the entire church, I ran up ahead to find another sculpture of Mary and the Christ child. This time, Mary was looking at her son, and the two of them were laughing. And I knew then I would always have them with me, and they were teaching me how to see.

12

of the sabbath

The word *Sabbath* conjures up images of sitting in the dark, in silence. Eating cold meals prepared the day before. Perhaps reading by candlelight. I have no idea why these pictures come to mind. Is it from my love of musical theater? Has Tevye formed my imagination and my theology of sparsity? I had read in Exodus, "Remember the Sabbath day by keeping it holy."[1] These scenarios seemed holy.

It wasn't until I experienced Sabbath with Benedictine monks that I understood: The Sabbath is holy. It is a day set apart, vastly different from the rest of the days of the week. But not in the way that I thought.

I'd been at the monastery for nearly a week before Sunday, the Sabbath. It was the quietest week I had ever known. It was the type of quiet so *loud* I could hear my stomach digesting. It was a noiselessness so still I heard the electricity buzzing through the wiring around me.

When I rose at 6:45 a.m., the monks had already prayed the hour of Vigils. I joined them for lauds, Mass, then the offices of terce, sext, none, vespers, and compline. When we prayed through the hours of the liturgy, I was usually the solitary lay person in the pews. The monks prayed in the quire, separated from me by a screen.

All my meals were taken alone. A tray of food was brought to me in the guest house dining room, and I ate to the ticking of an old clock. The meals were simple but nourishing: soup with bread and cheese, fish, and a bit of vegetables.

In the afternoons, I took long, wordless walks through voiceless forests and farmland. The only sounds were the crunching of my feet upon the cold earth below me.

As isolated as I was, I was not lonely. In all that silence, I heard God clearly. He spoke through the psalms from the liturgy that lingered in my mind and the sway of the trees in the woods. Everything was clean, ordered, and calm. It was the kind of quiet where you understand the psalm "Be still, and know that I am God."[2] There was a confidence that came with that silence. Clarity.

I nearly forgot it was Sunday as I put the tea things away in the guest house kitchen that morning until I heard cars pulling up for Mass. Car doors slammed. Families poured out of their vehicles and into the church. Children giggled and ran after each other. Men shook hands. Women hugged.

The organist popped into the guest house to say good morning before climbing the stairs to the grand organ above the nave. Her sturdy black shoes plodded up the stairs, and then the sound of music vibrated throughout the building for the first time that week.

Dom Andrew, my host monk, popped in too to let me

know tea and biscuits would be available after Mass and that my presence was desired. Parishioners wanted to know all about the woman from the States they had seen walking through their fields all week long.

I walked into the church, and it was the first time all week I couldn't sit in my regular spot, for the sanctuary was filled. Absolutely *jubilant*. After a week of silence, it felt like a party!

The first chords played on the organ for the processional hymn, and voices soared. I joined in, lifting my voice with my brothers and sisters, and my voice cracked. Spontaneous tears of joy streamed down my face.

I had not expected such overwhelming emotion to be in the midst of community—families with young children, elderly women with ancient coats around them, businessmen in their weekend casual, and the dear monks who had nurtured me all week long. What I had spent the week praying seemingly alone was now brought to beautiful fruition in this sea of song. I had a foretaste of heaven, what it will be like to worship God with the angels and saints and people just like you and me.

After Mass I joined the other parishioners for tea and biscuits. They were timid but curious about this American woman who had been staying with the monks and couldn't stop smiling. I met a couple from Poland who invited me to explore one of the land trusts, large aristocratic estates that were now owned by the government. And a woman who worked for a Catholic charity in the next town over offered me a ride into town for provisions the next day.

I talked to the monks I had prayed with and watched

beyond the screen all week. Dom John, who had cooked my delicious meals, told me about his mother, who worked in the textile mills of Manchester when he was a child. It was his father who stayed close to home with him and his siblings and taught him the basics of cooking. I talked to the abbot, a linguist, who spoke several languages and upon hearing I grew up in Los Angeles asked if Drew Barrymore had what he heard referred to as a "valley girl accent." I had never felt so exotic, but also I felt loved and cared for and connected in a way that can only be explained as the Spirit within us, honoring one another.

I slipped back into the guest house, my cheeks sore from smiling, when Dom John came in carrying lunch. Instead of the regular thoughtfully portioned fare, he came in with a tray with enough food for four: slices of roast beef, crispy potatoes, carrots, parsnips, peas, and Yorkshire pudding. My mouth fell open, aghast. "You're from the States," he said in his Manchester accent. "Well, this Sunday. You'll 'ave a *proper* Sunday roast." The plates filled the table. I was reminded of a song I used to sing as a child from the Song of Solomon: "He brings me to his banqueting table. His banner over me is love."[3] I did feel loved through all this food—by God and by the monks.

That lunch, I ate more than I had the whole week put together. When I thought I'd had my fill, Dom John returned with dessert—four types of cheeses, ripe figs, large globe grapes, and assorted crackers—and asked if I'd like some wine. I hadn't had wine in weeks. He filled an old crystal goblet with a deep red claret.

After all that food, I needed a nap. I laid down on my

guest room bed and thought about the abundance of the morning: the goodness of being with the family of believers and the overflowing bounty of a table. I only wished I could have combined the two, shared the table with the people. A decadent meal, like the Eucharist itself, is an anticipation of the marriage supper of the Lamb, when we will dine as guests of Christ.

I also couldn't help but realize that if I hadn't experienced the last quiet week of moderation, that Sunday would not have registered as abundance. At home, my schedule and my church are full of people. There is not space for the silence and solitude I experienced at the monastery. At home, my table is full, always. Frankly, I overeat. I rarely think of limiting my food or drink consumption. But in a week of fasting in different ways, I was able to see Sunday for what it is: a feast, a celebration, a mini resurrection, a little Easter, a foretaste of heaven. Holy.

13

in dreams of loss

Last night, I dreamed a dream so vivid and holy, I did not want to wake.

The dream was quotidian, mundane even: an evening sharing a meal and an after-dinner walk with you, my friend—but you've been gone for nearly twenty years now. But last night, you were alive and whole and happy.

I knocked on the door to your new apartment, the one you rented in Los Feliz after college. The one in the building from the 1920s with built-in shelves, coved ceilings, and arched doors. When you answered, you wore an apron, and your cats encircled my legs like baby tigers unsure of either play or prey. You beamed, just like you did that evening.

You poured us each a glass of wine, even though we weren't wine drinkers. It seemed like the thing to do when you are now grown up enough to have your own apartment and host dinner. The wine was frighteningly inexpensive white zinfandel, which both of us would be embarrassed to drink ten years later, had you lived ten more years.

You served salmon, asparagus, and couscous. I was so impressed you knew how to cook fish. We used both a fork *and* a knife, practicing our adult manners instead of using our thumbs to push food onto our forks. Neither of us had grown up with much. Our parents had clipped coupons and applied for aid to care for us. And now, here you were in this neighborhood, in this apartment, nicer than any home our parents had ever lived in.

We cleaned the kitchen together, telling stories of our high school years, when we wore mismatched clothes and made up fake languages that only we understood. We laughed so hard we thought we'd pee our pants, and then we remembered we ate asparagus, which made us laugh more, until we took turns using the bathroom.

After dinner we took a walk to look at the blooming bougainvilleas in your neighborhood. We walked into the hills, toward the observatory, where there were fewer apartments, more homes that dripped with old Hollywood and a time we longed for in our faded memories. You tried to find the house Stravinsky had lived in, and we vowed to listen to *The Firebird* when we returned to your apartment.

In the dream, but not that night, we walked arm in arm, like old ladies comfortable in our years of friendship, for this was before darkness and depression took over your mind—and took your life. We turned back to your apartment as the sun began to set and swore we saw an old movie star watering her lawn.

You served pie and decaf, but we didn't listen to *The Firebird* as intended; we chose Mahler's Symphony No. 2 instead, the one entitled "Resurrection." It begins as a funeral march but finishes with a chorus of saints and heavenly beings singing,

> You were not born in vain!
> You have not lived, suffered in vain!
> What came into being, it must cease to be!
> What passed away, it must rise again!
> Stop trembling!
> Prepare yourself to live![1]

Triumphant bells rang with the chorus. We listened that night as the music swelled hopefully, hinting at something beyond, something hallowed and indescribable.

It was time to go. But before I woke, I embraced you, smelled your hair, and held you longer than I ever did when you were here, when you were alive.

We did not know how happy we were back then. It is difficult to understand joy unless you have the contrast of hurt and sadness, of loss and pain.

I woke up sobbing—knowing you are really gone—and then sobbed with joy that for some reason, I got to spend my dream with you. Then I sobbed that I ever knew such a vivacious, curious, talented individual.

In Eastern Orthodox theology, remembering is to bring back the person, just for a moment—a little resurrection, a glimpse of the life to come when you will be even more whole and complete than that night in Los Feliz or in my dream.

I'm not afraid of life or of death. Nor of loss or of pain. For in the end, it is all a gift. It's only in hindsight that we know.

14

in a small moment: haircut

Mr. Chiang does not walk; he shuffles. I watch him from my window, and if I'm out in the yard, I holler hellooo, and he turns all shades of red, smiles, and gestures a floppy wave like a five-year-old instead of the septuagenarian he is. He walks away holding his hands behind his back, looking down at the ground. Humble. Meek.

I want to honor Mr. Chiang more, like the elder he is, but language gets in the way. He speaks Chinese. I do not.

I do, however, know his habits. I know he wears too-large khaki pants, and I am unsure if they ever did fit him snug. I know that in the mornings, he jogs the perimeter of the tiny city park down the street, then hangs from the children's monkey bars for a full minute, just hanging in traction, lengthening his body and spine for the day. I know he mows his lawn every other Thursday, and in the summer, he grows greens that he clips for dinner with scissors. And

I know he often buries some sort of root in a jar in his front yard. He is not secretive about this, but I like to imagine it is some sort of magic potion.

Mr. Chiang has lived across the street from me for over fifteen years. When we first moved in, Mr. Chiang had a college-aged son and Mrs. Chiang. His son has since moved away, married, had children, and built a successful military career that has taken him all over the world. And Mrs. Chiang, well, she died years ago. With each glimpse of her outside, we watched cancer melt her body away, until she did not come out of the house anymore.

I remember the day Mr. Chiang came to our fence with a piece of yellow lined paper with the number to a cab company. With broken English he asked my husband to call to schedule a pickup for Mrs. Chiang's doctor appointment in the morning. My husband drove them instead. He saw from the rearview mirror the pain in Mrs. Chiang's eyes each time he drove over a pothole or speed bump, even when he slowed the car to a crawl. When she was alive, she and Mr. Chiang wore matching gray utilitarian sweatpants while they did tai chi in the park. They moved and breathed in unison, but now it is just him.

It must be a lonely life, I think. My family reaches out with baked goods and a bounty when our apple-pear tree gives forth. Mr. Chiang is always grateful, smiles and nods, remembers us on Chinese New Year. But I think he understands loneliness differently than we do. He embraces it. He has his routine and his home and moves through life needing less than the rest of us. I think it is called contentment.

One routine I have not been able to figure out; it isn't

regular. It doesn't happen on the fifth Friday or the first of the month. About once a month, Mr. Chiang's brother comes over. The second Mr. Chiang is younger, a bit rounder at the edges, and has pants that fit. Rain or sun, the two of them pull a kitchen chair to the covered porch on the front of the house, and the two Mr. Chaings cut each other's hair.

This venture takes far longer than it should for two straightforward haircuts of elderly men with not much hair to begin with. The one cutting will don one of Mrs. Chiang's colorful aprons and drape a towel around the shoulders of the other. A comb, spray bottle, straight scissors, clippers, and brush for the back of the neck are involved. And they smile. Soft murmurs of conversation drift back and forth from brother to brother, and sometimes one will close his eyes, smile, and shake his head from side to side.

When I come upon the moment, it is always by surprise, never expected. I feel a sense of awe but also embarrassment—like perhaps I shouldn't look. I shouldn't see this gentle moment between elderly brothers. They are meticulous and tender. It is the happiest I see Mr. Chiang all month. And when I see it, I know something holy is happening.

15

confessions of a killjoy

If you were to peek into a copy of my sixth-grade yearbook, the one where I teased and hair-sprayed my bangs into a cascading waterfall, you'd find the words *Be Mature!* handwritten under my class photo. The words are there because I wrote them—on every single copy that was passed to me during class or out on the playground. When others were writing *2 good 2B 4gotten,* I was admonishing the eleven- and twelve-year-old set to grow up.

Why did I do this, you ask?

There is no easy way to say this.

I was a killjoy.

I'd like to tell you I got over this, but three years later, I scolded my best friend for wearing a costume on Halloween.

"We're in high school now. And Halloween is evil!" I said to her face as she stood there in a pink and gray 1950s poodle skirt and a pink cashmere sweater and a little scarf tied around her neck like Joanie Cunningham from *Happy Days.*

She rolled her eyes at me, pursed her lips, and said, "You know what you are? A killjoy. No one is allowed to have any fun—especially not you."

Looking back, I think I was a killjoy because responsibility had been thrust upon me at a young age. Parental neglect required that I learn quickly to take care of myself and care for my younger siblings. Being a killjoy justified this responsibility. And this responsibility meant I didn't know how to have fun.

But there is another reason why I donned the killjoy hat, and it is much more prideful. I thought, "How can I have the luxury of joy when there is war and famine, pain and injustice in the world?" As if dimming my emotions had any correlation to or control of the evils of the world.

Alexander Schmemann writes, "The knowledge of the fallen world does not kill joy, which emanates in this world always, constantly, as a bright sorrow."[1] Joy does not nullify suffering. On the contrary, it transforms suffering. Joy shines bright, takes power away from evil, and laughs in the face of deception and turmoil. "You will not take me!" joy says, shaking its fist. Because joy comes from outside oneself. It does not come from ourselves but from an act of surrender. Joy comes from surrendering oneself to God.

When my son was about three, I bought him some bright yellow puddle boots. I daydreamed about him walking about with an umbrella in hand saying, "Tut! Tut! It looks like rain!" in a little British accent like Christopher Robin. (But alas, we live in Seattle, and I married a Mexican.)

One day he walked to story time at the library in those boots. And of course, as one does in Seattle, he came upon a puddle and jumped right in without thought or hesitation. Why not? He was wearing puddle boots. Wasn't that the very thing they were for? But his mother, I, gave a stern, "Don't jump in puddles!" As soon as I heard myself say it, I thought, "Why the heck did I say that? Why do you give your kid shoes that you distinctly call 'puddle boots' only to tell him he can't do the very thing they were named for? I *am* a killjoy!"

I told the toddler I was sorry and that I shouldn't have said that. He shrugged it off easily, ignoring me as he splashed in puddle after puddle. That day, I made a point to schedule "puddle boot time." On a day when it had rained in the morning but was mild in the afternoon, which is nearly every day in Seattle, I bundled up my younger son in the stroller, had the toddler put on those bright yellow puddle boots, and we went out searching for a place to do their business.

My friend Starlene has known me since kindergarten and was once a recipient of my *Be Mature* yearbook. She knew me then, and she knows me now. Starlene's superpower is grace. She bestows it on everyone around her. As she watched me struggle with motherhood, reconciling my life as a killjoy, she said gently, "I'm sure God would have created the world very differently if he wanted us to be all business. Instead, he generously sprinkles opportunities to laugh and play and adore and savor."

I think of Starlene's sweetness during church when I hear words from the gospel of John. Christ says, "The thief comes only to steal and kill and destroy; I have come that they may have life, and have it to the full."[2] The thief does not only come to kill our bodies but also our spirit—to kill our joy. Christ wants just the opposite: abundance.

This is what I want: abundance. A life that is not merely living, but breathing, skipping, seeing, growing, delighting—and splashing.

16

# of letting God love you

I can't sit up.

It is not that I am physically incapable. But even the thought of sitting straight up in bed makes me want to sob. Sitting up is too much work, let alone actually getting out of bed.

Some use euphemisms to make this state more palatable, less gritty: the blues, a mental health day, a funk, the mean reds, melancholy.

But I have to be honest. This is depression.

If I look back on my life, I can tell you the years I lived in this state nearly every day. Then there was the year I simply tried to avoid it. I self-medicated. I rented a room in a city where no one knew me, and I drank often and copiously.

This depression doesn't happen that often anymore. But when it does, it is frightening. I know I am not going to be that person from that nameless year. But it is still terrifying. I don't want to be the person who simply lies in bed all day.

Today, I pull the blankets back over my head. I think of my to-do list for the day. It seems monumental. My body aches. Not because I am physically ill but from the tension I am holding. I whisper, "Help."

It is then that I remember what I learned that horrible year, the year of drinking and running and fighting. I learned that God loves me. There is nothing I can do to earn it. Not accomplishing my to-do list. Not getting out of bed. Nothing. He loves me. It is a gift. A grace.

In fact, if I just lie here all day long, God will still love me. And that is an astonishing thing to think about.

So I do. For a while.

I don't think I'd love me if all I did was lie here. I'm not sure there is anyone I'd love if they did nothing.

But God does.

Not only that, but he also doesn't love me because I love him. He loved me first. His love is not contingent on me loving him.

I think about that for a while.

All I have to do is let you love me.

To receive grace, the gift, the love.

So I do.

I lie there, and his love spreads over me like syrup on pancakes, like a hug when you needed one so badly, like a shower after you've been wearing the same clothes while camping in a mud puddle for a week, like the biggest present you didn't ask for and didn't know you needed and didn't realize you couldn't live without, until you pulled the ribbon and the box opened and—grace. That's the word. And until we feel it, we spend our whole life looking for it.

When I accept it, when I stop twisting and turning, his love heals and emboldens me.

This is how I healed from those years of depression in the first place. I had been trying to run away from him, trying to outrun God with alcohol and finding myself in bad situations.

But it was as if he were right behind me as I ran away. He pursued me. *Me!*

It was then that I simply gave up. *Fine. You can love me if you want.*

And I stopped running.

And he did love me.

That love healed me. Little by little.

Until I felt like I could do things I never thought I'd do: Go to seminary. Let a man love me. Have children.

I remember how far I've come. I don't want to be the person I was before. I don't want to fight his love again. I can at least sit up in bed.

When I let God love me, I want to love him back. I want to serve him in some way, to do something to show my love and appreciation.

○ ○ ○

When my husband and I first married, eager to find a system for our household, I said, "I washed the dishes, so why don't you do the laundry?" My husband looked at me, took me in his arms, smothered me with kisses, and said, "I'll do the laundry, but this isn't how we are going to live."

"What do you mean?" I asked, stupefied.

"We aren't going to make a list of tally marks of what you did and what I did and make sure they are even for twenty, thirty, forty years. That doesn't sound like a fun life."

He told me we were just going to do the things that needed to be done.

"I love you, so I want to pick up the clothes on the bathroom floor because I know it pleases you. It makes you happy. I don't do these things to even up the tally marks but because I love you."

I sank into his arms and thought about all these things he did for me. The thing was, he was being kind to me right then, because if we were to install some sort of tally system, I would be the one always on the short side. Always.

The kindness my husband and I share, the service to each other, is an outpouring of our love for one another.

○ ○ ○

It was my fault my ninety-one-year-old friend became emotional on the phone the other day.

We were talking about our fathers—his a hopeless drunk but also a man he always knew loved him. I found that contrast fascinating and one I could identify with. You see, my father too was a drunk, an addict of many vices, an abuser—but I know he loved me.

I told my friend that my father loved God too, very much. But despite this love for me and for God, my father could not accept God's love. He thought if he loved God enough, he could heal himself. My father didn't understand that the issue wasn't that he needed to love God more, but that he needed to allow God to love him.

I could hear my friend exhale on the other end of the line. "Please forgive me; I'm a bit emotional," he said. "That's beautiful and so true."

Understanding that God loves me and accepting that love is how I could forgive my father. It is how I have empathy for a man who stalked and psychologically tormented me for years, a man whose definition of love was so warped and confused, he acted it out in bizarre, unhealthy ways. And it's how I was able to see what true love is.

Surrendering myself to God's love is how I am able to see the world through a lens of joy and love.

I thought about this on a recent trip with my middle school–aged son. I have broken the cycle that my father continued from those before him and am a good and loving mother. It was bliss to show my son beautiful things and introduce him to new knowledge about his place in the world. My son lit up when he saw sheep on our walks in the countryside or a painting he had seen once in a book now before him in person, or had an interaction with a stranger that made him feel more a part of the world.

My son and I talked about how God enjoys giving us gifts, how God shows us beautiful things and introduces us to new ideas and knowledge to amuse us, to expand our view. Just like a good mommy, God, a good father, loves to delight us. When we allow God to love us, we can see those gifts he has set out to dazzle us.

As my elderly friend and I shared stories on the phone, we discovered we share this outlook on life—one of gratitude and amazement at the goodness we've been allowed to see.

The following anonymous quote is often incorrectly attributed to Clare of Assisi, but I still think it's a worthy sentiment: "We become what we love, and who we love shapes what we become." Being loved by Christ shapes who I am and who I am becoming. I know that even if I just lie in bed all day, he will still love me. There are days when I have done just that, but today I will sit up, get out of bed, love my family. Even the silly little things on my to-do list become acts of love, of worship to the One who loves me.

17

of compline

When I was a child, it was difficult to fall asleep. Every sound, within and without, carried me out of sleep. I was curious. Shadows from passing cars and trees as wind blew through them danced across my wall. I got the sense that what happened at night was more real than what I saw during the day. And that it wasn't all benevolent.

I often felt something evil in my room. When I tell people this, they think I merely had an active imagination as a child, but it was more than that. It was a true dark presence. I couldn't see it, but I could feel it.

Once, when my father tucked me in at night, I confided in him about the evil I often felt in the room after he closed the door. My father didn't look at me like grown-ups do now when I tell this story, as if I am strange or simple or have grown into some sort of silly woman. He did not flinch. He looked me straight in the eye as if he understood the severity of this presence.

My father taught me what would be the first Scripture

I ever memorized: "God hath not given us the spirit of fear; but of power, and of love, and of a sound mind."[1] He told me the evil I sensed was not from God. But if I called upon God, just his name would frighten the darkness.

"You have this power in you, Shemaiah. Don't be afraid to use it," he said as he left the room.

I lay turning the words over in my head. I whispered the names I knew for God and the Scripture my father taught me until I fell into a deep sleep.

The darkness did not come that night. But it would. And when it did, I was ready.

I felt it one night, in the corner of the room like a rabid rat ready to climb up my bedpost and pounce. I sat bolt upright in bed, fearless, and declared, "You are not welcome here. In the name of Jesus, go away."

And it did. But I want to tell you how. I want you to know how sane and clear I was then, and am now, and that this was not the only time this happened, so I know it is true and right and real.

When I said those words, it was as if something else—something that was already there, though I hadn't realized it—expanded. Like a balloon, it filled itself until it swelled, was swollen, taking up all the space until that diseased creature in the corner was squeezed right out of my bedroom.

And I knew it was real. Goodness itself was right there in the room with me. Love and joy and peace and all that was good and right and true was there, loving me, protecting me.

I have never lost the sense that at night something more real happens than what I see during the day.

○ ○ ○

In *The Catholic Catalogue,* a marvelous book written by a mother and daughter team, Melissa Musick and Anna Keating explain all the small daily acts that add together to make up a holy life. They speak of nighttime as a "hinge moment" in which "a door swings open on its hinges to reveal whatever is waiting on the other side."[2] I grasp this as an understanding of the words in creeds that say we believe in things seen and unseen. Yes, I do believe there is a reality we cannot see.

Children seem to understand this more than grown-ups. Musick and Keating write that bedtime is a "loss of consciousness and control" that is in its own way "a little death."[3] This can "be frightening," they write, "which is why we adults so often anesthetize ourselves with alcohol, drugs, or television."[4] This observation hits too close to home as I enjoy my nightly martini and a few hours of BBC dramas. I never stopped to think of how the horror of childhood bedtime stayed with me. This makes the classic children's prayer "Now I Lay Me Down to Sleep" even more daunting. Many find the lines

> If I should die before I 'wake,
> I pray the Lord my Soul to take.

traumatizing, but I think sensitive children like me appreciate these words to protect our souls.

Benedictine monks understand this "little death" and the darkness that comes with nightfall. During my weeklong stay at the abbey in England, I learned to long for the Daily Office of compline, the last prayers of the day.

The Benedictines do not fuss with language as I do. They are unconcerned with whether someone will find them strange or simple. One of the Scriptures for this office is "Be sober, be watchful. Your adversary the devil prowls around like a roaring lion, seeking some one to devour. Resist him, firm in your faith."[5] The Benedictines are familiar with the rabid rat I sensed in the corner of the room and who he works for.

While our toothbrushes lay by our sinks, waiting to be used, we chanted together in a candle-lit church to the tune of a traditional Welsh melody,

> Dark descends, but light unending
> Shines through our night.[6]

The monks left the quire where they pray in order to stand in a half circle in the nave where I prayed. The abbot reached for holy water and sprinkled each man as they girded themselves for sleep. He would not forget me, and as I felt the sweet water splash against my forehead, I made the sign of the cross, in gratitude for the Lord's protection.

Our eyes grew soft as we began to fade, ready for slumber, rest for our bodies and spirits. But before we left the church, we prayed,

> Lord may your love be with us while we sleep
> And your strong care our souls and bodies keep
> Lord may your truth inform our minds always,

> And may your spirit turn our night to day
> Lord may your peace be in our hearts held fast,
> Bring us in safety home to you at last[7]

My host monk walked me back to my quarters in the guest house. I was the only guest that night, and the monk locked the big heavy Victorian door with a skeleton key so the entire perimeter of the church was secure and safe.

He whispered good night and left on the hall light *so I shan't trip should I need to use the loo in the middle of the night.* He told me Saint Benedict wrote in his rule to always keep a light on in the hallway at night. "He wasn't just spiritual; he was practical too," the monk whispered, smiling.

As I lay in bed after compline, I caught a glimpse of God's glory, especially how God the Father had protected me and loved me through the words and actions of the monks that evening. Tucked in bed, I was enveloped in God's peace and love. I knew I'd sleep well, but I also thought I understood more clearly the words of the psalmist:

> even the darkness will not be dark to you;
> the night will shine like the day,
> for darkness is as light to you.[8]

The goodness of God was present with me in the abbey guest house. Love and joy and peace and all that was good and right and true was there, loving me, protecting me.

I rested in joy, and I knew I'd rise in it too.

18

# of knowing you are small

It was one of those perfect Northwest summer mornings. We woke early, our steaming coffees in hand as we drove out of the city and into the mist of the Cascade Mountain Range. We hiked till noon. Our legs moved strong and sturdy under us as we gained altitude and confidence. As the sun rose higher in the sky, it shone down dappled through the forest covering, and when we finally reached the summit, the mist had broken, and we could see the land stretched out for miles.

We knew once we were home we would remember what we'd seen from above. We saw where we lived from on high. We wondered if this is how eagles or astronauts or God himself feels as he looks down upon us.

We heard Walt Whitman's own answer echo in our heads:

> That you are here—that life exists and identity,
> That the powerful play goes on, and you may
> contribute a verse.[1]

We were small but satisfied to be part of that landscape.

Our bodies, sunned and solid, descended back to the car, where we were no longer eagles or astronauts or gods but his offspring in which "we live and move and have our being."[2] And as we drove home, we felt we understood more clearly G. K. Chesterton's words, "How much larger your life would be if your self could become smaller in it."[3]

That's when we saw the roadside stand boasting of Rainier cherries straight from the tree. We bought a bag to share on the ride home. They were still warm with the sun itself. Sweet, juicy, tart, and luscious. We spit the seeds out the car windows onto the country roads like children.

We said aloud, "We are happy. We are happy!" so we would not forget.

19

trumpet joy

When my son was eight, the FedEx man delivered a very large and heavy box with my son's name on it the week before Christmas. The return address named his adult cousin as the sender. My son was all shades of excitement because his cousin has muscles and looks like the Hulk, except he isn't green but a nice shade of brown, so he looks like the Mexican Hulk, which in my son's eyes is a better superhero idea, especially since he actually knows the Mexican Hulk, his cousin.

It was difficult to wait till Christmas morning to open the box, but when he did, it revealed his cousin's old marching band trumpet. I hadn't seen eyes that shiny on Christmas morning since my little sister opened her coveted Cabbage Patch doll. It took us all about three seconds to realize that trumpet lessons were in our near future.

Those first few months of lessons were tough. Not for him—he loved the lessons and even loved practicing. But the rest of us were constantly on edge. At any moment he might belt out a shrill note, not unlike a call to battle from the *Lord of the Rings* films. Each one sent shivers up my spine. I thought maybe I should look to the clouds just in case it was the second coming, but there he would stand, cheeks pink with glee, oblivious to the sudden barrage of barking dogs in our neighborhood.

I would rummage through cabinets to see if there was something to take off the edge—a long-lost bottle of Valium or a shot of tequila—but all we had was a box of peppermint tea. I'd holler out a "That sounds so good, baby!" as my hands shook putting on the kettle.

Good thing we all stuck it out, because the kid got good. I mean real good. By the time he was ten, it was clear that this kid had a different rhythm deep down inside him—the kind of rhythm where it seems like Thelonious Monk is going to miss the note when he slaps the keys on the piano with those huge mitt hands of his, but he hits it half a second later than you would have, and it is perfection, nay, genius. And you realize jazz musicians are made up of something completely different from you and me. It's the kind of rhythm that makes singing along with Frank Sinatra impossible; his phrasing is unique to him. We learn we are graced to be around instruments such as these.

This is what is going on in my kid. I'm not saying this just because I'm his mother or because we have the same soul-searching eyes and fiery tempers. This kid can play. I mean, he *swings*. He blows, bounces, and blips like he was born in the wrong decade. He squeezes his lips for those high notes. He gets his horn to purr in those low jungle growls. He even harmonizes with the melody.

My son was eleven when COVID lockdowns hit Seattle. He took it upon himself to entertain our housebound eighty-five-year-old neighbor. He marched over to her house like some sort of reverse Pied Piper and played the old standard "Don't Get Around Much Anymore" from the sidewalk in front of her house. The rest of the neighborhood howled in laughter at the appropriate choice in song, but he was oblivious.

If you tried to tell this kid how good he is, he'd shrug or roll his eyes or tell you it's easy and you could do it if you really wanted to, that he doesn't even like playing the trumpet, it's just something he does. But I see how lost he gets in the repetition, in the beat, in the call and response. My son isn't going to be the next Louis Armstrong, but he is most himself when he plays.

Many consider the trumpet the happiest of instruments, and this is mostly due to Louis Armstrong himself. The trumpet was an extension of Armstrong, and when he played, he was the most Louis he could be. Composer and conductor Leonard Bernstein said of Armstrong, "What he does is real, and true, and honest, and simple, and even noble. Every time this man puts his trumpet to his lips, even if only to practice three notes, he does it with his whole soul."[1]

When Louis Armstrong played, it sounded as if his trumpet played a message from God himself to remind you that even though you may be poor or sad or ugly or a sinner, he sees value in you and wants you to see all the good things he has waiting for you. That grace exists all around you—ready for the taking.

Put in your earbuds and listen to Armstrong play "West

End Blues." The first twelve seconds will change your life. How can he play each of those notes so clean and clear? And when he hits the high note, you know—*know* in your bones, down your spine—that God exists and that he is good.

When you hear Armstrong play the blues, which he knew well, as he grew up in a New Orleans brothel where his mother was a prostitute, you have the sense that everything is going to be okay. We are going to make it out, and we'll be even stronger than before.

Joy knows pain. One must know the depths of struggle to know the elation of joy. We need people who have known both to show us the way out, to give us hope.

Perhaps this is what I see in my son, a rhythm all his own, the ability to be completely himself. In this act of being "real, and true, and honest, and simple, and even noble," he paves the path for others. Some guide us through art or words, laughter or dance. My son, like Armstrong, uses music to show a neighborhood there are no walls holding us in, but rather that our concert hall has simply expanded. He shows us how to be who we truly are: the people God created us to be . . . the most ourselves.

20

of oranges

Never rush to peel an orange. If someone happens to be sitting near as you break the flesh with your thumbnail, invite them to inhale the initial spray of citrus as a gift. The scent calms as it cheers.

Slowly, languidly, attempt to peel the rind in one long singular strand. Bonus points if you can take that strand and re-form it into a hollow orange. If anything, it will make you smile.

Gently gather each string of pith from the outer edges of your orange. This requires patience, but patience tastes better than haste.

Tenderly pull each segment away from the cluster. Each one is an edible jewel. When you place it in your mouth, it will explode with equal parts sweet and tart.

Once, at the Asheville airport, a group of poets invited me to share in their bounty of clementines. Each bite reminded us of poems we had stored in our memory. We took turns reading these treasured poems aloud to each other. These poems served as benedictions before we parted ways, each to a flight for a different part of the country.

In high school, each year, my English teacher read a poem about first love, sacrifice, and oranges to his incoming class. He couldn't read the poem without his voice cracking as he struggled not to cry during the last two lines. It became an annual joke to ask the freshmen if he cried reading "Oranges," but now I too can't read that poem without breaking, both for the beauty of the poem and the mark left by that sweet teacher who taught us how to see, even if the lens would take us years to look through.

Today I taught a little girl who is not my own how to peel an orange. She watched with curious and expectant eyes. She was not in a hurry for her snack. She knew I was showing her more than what she could see.

21

# of favorite pants

I hope you have a pair of favorite pants, because I do.

Mine are red, black, and green plaid—and they are *everything*! They look like pajama bottoms, at least to my children, who were not around in the 1970s and '80s when people wore things like this without irony. Yet these pants are fitted, slimming, and tailored. To be even more precise, they are a bit snug. When I wear them, I imagine this must be what it felt like to be an actor on *Star Trek*, where they couldn't eat anything solid on filming day lest the bodysuit, which was probably sewn onto them, would burst.

Each fall when I pull these pants out of the storage box, I say a little prayer that they still fit. I hold my breath the first time I zip them up, and if they fit, I immediately text my closest friends a photo of the pants saying, "Did you miss me?" I know these pants are a little bit too much; they are tight and ostentatious and a little intense, just like me.

"The Pants," as I will hereby refer to them, come out as soon as the weather turns crisp—so, say, around the first week of October. But since they do have a Christmassy vibe to them, I try not to wear them past the twelve days of Christmas, or I'll look silly.

Understand, the window for wearing these pants is very limited, perhaps even shorter than the white pants I can wear only in the summer. *But I'm not talking about those pants right now!* Those aren't even in my top five favorite pants.

But The Pants are reminiscent of my high school years, when I wore strange clothing combinations. When I would experiment with my look. When I was discovering who I was going to be. Thank goodness The Pants stuck and not the shapeless, woven, heavy-as-a-Persian-rug, Joseph-and-the-Amazing-Technicolor-Dreamcoat of a dress my friend brought back from a mission trip to Guatemala. The Pants are fallish, holidayish, and maybe a little bit punk rock.

I wear them because they remind me not to gorge myself on Halloween candy and holiday cookies and that, despite what people say, pumpkin spice lattes do have calories. But I also wear them to remind myself not to take myself too seriously. I have grown up enough to embrace the intense and ostentatious me. And that I can be silly too. And that life is for living.

22

of Costco

I started going to Costco for the diapers. Well, I'll back up a bit.

My friend Carl looked at my stuffed-sausage-of-a-stomach and said, "You're going to need a Costco membership."

It seemed like an odd thing to say to someone in their last month of pregnancy, but I bit.

"Why?" I asked.

"You are going to want to buy your diapers there. They are cheaper. We'll go on a double date on Saturday."

This was my introduction to Costco: on a double date with my husband and Carl and his partner, Mario. We had recently moved to Seattle. We had no family in the city and few friends. Now I was gleefully pregnant but beginning to feel a little overwhelmed. Carl worked with my husband, saw my pregnant tummy, and decided to take me under his wing. I am forever grateful.

We went to Costco on the busiest day and time, Saturday morning. Carl drove us there. He had a game plan. He was going to walk us through the entire store and *introduce us to everyone,* and then we'd grab a hot dog or a slice of pizza for lunch.

I didn't understand what he meant by "introduce us to everyone" until we arrived and learned that Carl knew everyone, and everyone knew Carl. He introduced me to the lady who checked membership cards at the door, tapped on the glass to wave at the butchers, hollered to the guy moving pallets on the forklift, talked shop with the wine guy, and of course, stopped at every single sample cart. Carl walked us down every aisle. He showed me where the diapers were, and the vitamins, as I would certainly need them in my postpartum care, and the produce, for salad packs that would be easy to eat for lunch when I was home alone with the baby when my husband returned to work after paternity leave. After a $1.50 hot dog and soda lunch, I was sold.

It was the first outing I took my son on after he was born. I simply did what Carl did. I said hello to everyone. I didn't realize how odd this was. I thought that was the vibe of the store. No, it was just Carl's vibe. But especially since I had a baby in tow, people responded to me in an open, welcoming way.

What I didn't realize then that I know now is I was looking for connection and community, and I strangely found it at Costco. Carl showed me the way.

Costco became a major weekly outing for baby and me every Thursday morning. Since I came at the same time each week, I noticed other shoppers on the same schedule too. Theresa, who worked at my church, came with the church van to buy provisions for the weekend activities.

The woman with the short black hair gave me a curt nod of recognition. And the older man with his Navy ball cap gave me a big smile.

I made connections with employees too. Tony liked to make both the baby and me giggle by breaking through boxes like he was a monster. Ceya began giving me a hug every week. I thought this was because she discovered I was a Christian like herself. She'd always call me sister and stop whatever she was doing to give me a hug. Most weeks, exhausted and lonely, I really needed a hug. I later discovered Ceya does this to all the regulars. She has a ministry of hugs. Ron, a checker, was patient and kind, and I began to check out only in his line. For those three minutes, I felt connected and seen as he rang up my strawberries and ground beef and asked me about my week and my baby. Tom checked my receipt at the door and guessed within an impressive five dollars how much I spent each week. Employees and shoppers alike cooed at my son in his infant carrier, until he had to sit in the cart itself and my next pregnancy began to show. Soon I had an infant and a toddler in the double-seated cart.

Like Carl showed me, I taught my boys how to navigate Costco. It was a necessary outing each week; why not make it fun?

Dragon fruit juice for $3.99 a gallon? I have no idea what a dragon fruit is, but let's try it out. Pork chops are on sale for $1.99 a pound? It's pork chop week! Twenty pairs of socks for $19.99? I think my husband's sock drawer needs an overhaul. A vat of chocolate-covered almonds for $14.99? Look who's having a party after I put these babies to sleep! And of course, I'm not leaving without a $4.99 chicken.

Sometimes the next holiday isn't even on my radar, but Costco makes sure I'm thinking about it. Halloween costumes in July. Christmas wrapping paper out on the floor on the last day of September. And as soon as spring break is a memory, flats of fireworks are available for purchase. Costco reminds me there is always something to look forward to on the calendar.

When my sons started school, Costco was where I'd get my baby fix. Missing my growing boys, but certainly not wanting or needing any more children, I watched what I call "the baby parade"—carts of mothers and babies and babies and fathers throughout the store. If a babbling, slobbery kid smiled at me, *bonus!* The rest of my day was going to be awesome.

Once, I overheard a one-year-old ask his mom, aisle after aisle, where the butter was. She patiently responded, seven or seventy times, "Not this aisle." When they finally got to the butter fridge, the mother took out a brick of Kirkland butter and handed it to the toddler in the front seat of the cart. He held the butter like a baby, gently patting it and caressing it until they reached the checkout. I couldn't stop laughing. "He does this every time," the mother told me, straight-faced as she watched him plant a kiss on the cube.

I'll never forget a mother and her large family moving through the aisles. Her son, around thirteen, pushed the cart while his youngest brother lay on the rack under the basket. A daughter around eleven pushed her younger sister in a wheelchair as the mom called out items on the list to chuck into the cart. The mother looked tired but happy, and after a few aisles trailing after them, I caught up with them. "I just wanted to tell you guys," I said, looking each of them in the eye, "that I've been watching you, and you have incredible teamwork. What a family!" The mom got a little misty-eyed and whispered thank you, then straightened up and said, "Did you hear that? Go team Willis!" She high-fived each of her kids. They beamed, bolstered.

At Costco you see a panorama of humanity: An elderly couple discussing the merits of purchasing a meal kit. An East African man working an Instacart list, pushing the flat-bed cart down the aisles like he's in a video game. A Filipino family working in a group of nearly ten, with two carts. A Muslim woman with her cell phone tucked inside her hijab so she can talk hands-free while she shops.

Once, knee-high wellies were on sale for half the retail price. (In Seattle, you need a good pair of boots.) I searched the stacks for my size, 9, and when I pulled the boots out, a woman caught up in the frenzy of a good buy said, "Oh good! Size 9," and grabbed them out of my hands. Her husband looked at her and looked at me, and we all started laughing at the same time. "I am so sorry!" she said, giving the boots back to me. I told her I understood the excitement of a good deal and helped her find another size 9. I sat down on the floor to try on my pair, but when I went to take them off, I realized I couldn't. They were stuck on. The woman saw my dilemma and told her husband, who was closer to me, "Pull her boot off!" There I was, lying on the floor of Costco with some strange man trying to pull the boot off my thick calf. The woman and I laughed so hard we had tears streaming down our faces.

I recently read a social media post explaining that many

people have not returned to the office after the pandemic, preferring to work from home. Many no longer go to church or belong to clubs either. Costco has become a gathering place. There, you see the parent from your daughter's kindergarten PTA or your old dentist over by the smoked salmon sample cart. Or see people lingering near the book tables to talk with a past coworker. Or overhear a merry cry as two old friends see each other in the produce aisle.

Just last week I passed the frozen pizzas and nearly ran my cart into the mother of our old babysitters. This woman has six children, and we moved through the roster as each child phased out of babysitting and into college. My fourteen-year-old was with me that day, and for a moment we both remembered her children at this age, knocking on the door on a Friday night so my husband and I could go out on a date. My son did not remember the mom, but he certainly remembered her son who had built a leprechaun trap out of toilet paper rolls and egg cartons from the recycling. Her son had snuck back to the trap after the children went to sleep and put his own pocket change in the trap. In the Costco aisle, we connected again over these stories of her sweet sons, now out of the house building their own lives.

I no longer need diapers for my sons, but I may one day need them for myself. Those are in aisle 3. As I get closer to those years, I remember my last birthday, when my favorite cashier, Ron, who has now become a friend outside of Costco—we spend holidays together—announced my birthday in the employee morning meeting. When I arrived to shop that morning, nearly every employee wished me a happy birthday as I moved through the store. Ceya stopped the forklift to give me an extra birthday hug. Tony gave me a high five as he passed through after his break. The man giving out samples mentioned mine was free since it was my birthday. And the guy who stacks carts outside, the one with an actual feather in his cap, sang to me. He sang loud and strong and clear, in front of all the shoppers and cars and carts in the parking lot. Who needs a party when you have Costco?

23

in daydreaming

My interior life is not an easy thing to convey to my husband or sister or friends, let alone a stranger. One way to try to explain it is that I daydream. Copiously. Extensively. Considerably. A lot.

I always have.

When I was young, I daydreamed about houses. I imagined walking through vast Victorians or mod mid-centuries. Each door opened to something marvelous. A door might reveal a library, warm with the glow of a fireplace, filled floor to ceiling with shelves of books. I perused titles, often choosing based on the size or color of the cover. Then I curled up on the hearth, tucked into my pile.

Another door opened to a nook built into the wall. An old-fashioned telephone, the kind with one piece to speak into and another to listen, lived inside the nook. I lifted the receiver and listened to two women having a conversation on a party line. It wasn't anything salacious or improper, just two women sharing the details of their day and family.

Another door opened to a girl's bedroom. The window seat revealed that it was on the second story. Along one wall was a white brass daybed with a pink-and-blue flowered Laura Ashley comforter. The other wall was lined with candy dispensers, similar to ones in a bulk candy store. The containers were arranged by color so that it appeared as a candy rainbow across the wall: jelly beans, orange slices, lemon drops, and cherry sours ready for feasting.

There was also a dining room. A table with seating for twelve took up most of the room and overflowed with gorgeous linens, exquisite china, and food fit for a king: bottles of wine, nuts—whole, still inside the shell—bunches of grapes, and roasted fowl.

I dreamed these daydreams when I finished my class assignments and got lost staring outside the classroom window; or when reading in a closet, a frequent hideaway for me; or in the back seat of the car while my parents ran errands. I'd annoy my parents, teachers, and friends by not responding to my name until repeated for perhaps the third time.

It would be years before I understood these daydreams. Prayer and therapy revealed that these dreams were my desire for a home. I can see now that they all imitated scenes I had seen in films or read in books. Yet there were never people in these daydreams, just me and an immense quiet house. My parents were neglectful, poor, and abusive. I knew I would not feel safe with them in this dream. It would be just a house, not a home.

Daydreaming reveals our deepest desires, our values, and our heart. Where our dreams lie, there too lies our joy—the way we connect with our Creator.

I still daydream. Often it happens when I am in the shower or blow-drying my hair or doing the dishes. The white noise sends me to a different place.

Letting your mind wander is a luscious luxury. I imagine I'm sitting on a hill in Scotland, the wind rippling through my hair, cutting through the woolen fisherman's sweater, as I watch black-faced sheep move through the pasture below. I shield my eyes from the sun as it peeks from behind the clouds, dusting the grass gold. I inhale. The air smells of earth and sea and smoke from a woodpile beyond.

I was there. For two minutes I sat on that hill. My breath quieted, my blood pressure lowered, and the tenderest expression spread across my face. If anyone had found me in this state, they would have thought I was in love, for that is no doubt what it looked like, unadulterated love.

There is something about a daydream that leaves you naked. You spill all the secrets of your heart for a moment, that which you desire and long for. Is it not much different than prayer? In daydreaming we lay out our desires, hopes, and fears before God. In daydreaming we are vulnerable.

I think my Scottish daydream is about longing for presence. While the hum of my dryer whispers in my ear, I am sitting with God in stillness, looking over his majestic creation. This daydream becomes worship.

Daydreaming as prayer might seem far-fetched to some, but it was in daydreams that Saint Ignatius found Christ. When a cannonball shattered his legs, ending his military career, Inigo was laid up in recovery for months. Wracked with pain and without mobility, Inigo had little to do but read and daydream. When he asked for books to be brought to his bed, instead of the romantic novels with tales of El Cid and Camelot, his caretakers brought him a *Life of Christ* and *Lives of the Saints.*

When he wasn't reading, he indulged in daydreaming. At first he reminisced of battles and women, but soon the books painted the pictures of his inner life. He dreamed of service, not to the king of Spain but to Christ the King. Through these daydreams he searched for God until he realized God was right there with him.

I asked my friend John if he thought I was kooky for thinking my daydreams could be prayers. "How else could it be possible to pray without ceasing?" he answered so matter-of-factly that I realized I was silly for even asking the question.

Sometimes my interior life is much richer and more real than my outer life—than the pile of shoes by our front door and the dishes that lie in wait in the sink. And sometimes that interior life affects my outer life, making it richer and more real as Christ fills my desires, hopes, and dreams. Christ answered those prayers for a home. My house is not vast; it is small but cozy. This one-hundred-year-old house with its paper-thin walls and leaky basement is the only one my children have ever known. We have filled it with books but also celebrations—of holidays and birthdays, of sacraments, and yes, of restored health and dried tears. It is not just a house. It is a home.

24

in food

My friend Katie calls to check in and go over logistics the day before she and her family are to fly out from the East Coast to Seattle to visit.

"I just want to sit and eat and talk," she tells me.

I know what she means. This is what we do when we get together. Our husbands have forged a friendship of nearly twenty-five years of cooking together. Sure, they share politics and faith, but before visiting each other, the men text about what they want to *cook*.

Katie and I find a spot to lounge and chat while our children play, until charcuterie boards simply appear before us. These boards are works of art. Prosciutto and mortadella nestle up against dried apricots and French triple cream that was set out to ripen so that now it spreads on artisan rosemary crackers like butter. Spanish Marcona almonds encircle our latest favorite, a spicy savory tomato jam.

A luscious pinot noir is placed into our hands. We swirl the glasses languidly as it is the only exercise we will be performing today. And these, my friends, are only the appetizers. For dinner, our husbands will search for an enormous steak the size of an atlas or an overnight bag. Or perhaps they will decide to make homemade raviolis stuffed with fresh crab served with farm peas and mint.

When the main course is ready, the men and the children, and often a friend or two we've called to join, will fill up the table, and we'll sit. And eat. And talk.

What do we talk about? Mostly we talk about other amazing meals we've had together, or apart.

Like one of the first times we ate with Katie. It was just a few years after she and her husband married. We met at a restaurant in DC. The menu boasted a roast duck that served two but let the diner know the duck would take over an hour to cook. We hadn't even ordered drinks when Katie set down her menu and asked who would share the roast duck with her. We knew we were in for a long, luxurious meal and loved Katie right there and then. She was our kind of people.

○ ○ ○

I did not always have this abundance in my life. When I was growing up, my family was poor.

I remember going to the grocery store with my mother and two younger sisters. I was in charge of "the clicker," a plastic handheld tally to keep track of how much we were spending. We could not go over the amount of government-issued food stamps for the week. If we did, the cashier at the checkout line would let us know. That would bring double the embarrassment, first of going over and then of having to decide what needed to go back—while everyone watched.

We purchased basics covered by the food stamps, which seemed to be mostly starches. Our big splurge was milk. My mother despised the powdered milk offered and instead indulged on a gallon of real milk.

Some families knew how to make the basic ingredients offered by the government into something delicious. I visited homes that had only beans, cheese, and tortillas, but the mom could make fifty different delicious meals out of those three ingredients. My mother, Lord bless her, was not one of those moms. The food of my childhood was a lot of gray, flavorless hamburger patties and fried potato slices.

We rarely ate together as a family. Looking back, I can't conjure up one image of my mother eating. Certainly not at our home, and certainly not at our kitchen table. Usually just my sisters and I sat at the table. There was always tension. Would my father come to dinner? Or would he have already eaten? He usually ate elsewhere—take-out food on the job or on the way home. But even when he wasn't there, his presence loomed. He was intimidating and unpredictable and blew much of our grocery budget on his vices.

Now when I sit down to eat delicious food with my friends and family, I am breaking a cycle of distrust and abuse, scarcity and hostility. I feel connected to the people at the table in a way I was never allowed as a child. I see that this food isn't nourishing only our bodies but also our spirits.

○ ○ ○

Not all meals need to be lavish to connect. One of my favorite childhood meals, one I have shared with my sons many times, was a weekend lunch with my best friend's family when I was about eight.

My parents fought often. When they fought, or when they were trying to patch things up, they dropped me and my sisters at the Romeros for the weekend.

This family struggled with money and life as we did, but they always took us in. The Romeros had three children, and the six of us would play Legos and ride bikes and put on elaborate variety shows for anyone who would watch.

One weekend, my parents dropped us off when Mrs. Romero was out of town on a women's retreat with church. Mr. Romero still took us in, even saying it would be easier now that his kids had friends to play with. After a morning of playing hard in the neighborhood, we returned, sweaty, dirty, and ravenous, hoping to find lunch.

Mr. Romero looked in the cupboards and found a jumbo can of tuna and a loaf of bread. It wasn't enough for all seven of us, but he had an idea. We would cut up every vegetable we could find into tiny bits and add it to the tuna. We hoped it would stretch enough to feed us all.

My best friend and I were in charge of cherry tomatoes from their garden. We picked, washed, and cut them into fourths. There were carrots and celery left in the crisper. The two youngest got to dicing those, and Mr. Romero used it as a teaching moment, training them to use a knife. The oldest Romero son chopped up half a head of purple cabbage, and my sister set the table.

Someone said our tuna looked like a rainbow with all the

colors inside. Mr. Romero added mayo and spices and spread out sandwiches for us all. He said it was like the loaves and the fishes in the Bible, but with StarKist and Wonder Bread. We all laughed. It was the most delicious tuna I ever had in my entire life, then and since, because we had all helped make it and felt like we had witnessed a little miracle.

○ ○ ○

It's a shame the table of my childhood couldn't have been a place for transcendence.

"The world begins at a kitchen table. No matter what, we must eat to live," poet Joy Harjo writes in her poem "Perhaps the World Ends Here." The table is sacred. It is where "children are given instructions on what it means to be human."[1]

I want to go back in time and whisper into my mother's ear, "This is where you can save us." We wanted so much to learn how to be women—to cook, to love, and to choose men different from the one who left us so hungry.

I now have an aversion to cooking. After years of poverty and friction, cooking gives me great anxiety, but I cherish eating in a way that only a child of poverty can.

It is no small thing to sit and eat together. At a table, among people and food, our dreams rise to the surface. These dreams become food or friend, sitting at the table with us. I believe it deep in my heart. My mother had no dreams for us. She was too busy just trying to survive. And I understand.

My husband dreamed for me instead. After knowing me for thirteen years, he asked me out, and on that first date, he created a petite amuse-bouche—"Something to make your mouth happy," he said as he popped it into my mouth before dinner. He drizzled deep dark chocolate on endive spears, nestling a morsel of blue cheese and a crack of caramelized walnut within each curl. I was incredulous: *Chocolate on lettuce?* Yet the bite unlocked something inside me. Something I had never known before. The complementary textures and flavors detonated inside me. I looked at his expectant face as he waited to see if I enjoyed the bite. The attention he gave to one bite . . . for me. I knew he loved me.

It took me a while to love him back. I didn't know how. And I was scared to. But this man kept feeding me. In time, I learned that at the table he prepared for me there was enough space for my fear and hesitation and hunger.

It is at the table that there is space to hold it all—sadness, love, fear, and hope. This is where life can be transformed from merely fuel and surviving, to nourishment and thriving.

○ ○ ○

Perhaps you've seen the exquisite icon *The Holy Trinity* painted by fifteenth-century Russian painter Andrei Rublev. It portrays the scene in Genesis 18 when three mysterious guests visit Abraham and Sarah. With abundant hospitality, the couple wash the visitors' feet and serve them a meal. When the guests tell the couple that Sarah, who is nearly ninety, will bear a son by the same time next year, the couple realizes these guests are angels.

These three beings speak and act in complete unity with one another. Early Christians understood this Old Testament story and icon as a revelation of the Holy Trinity, the three persons within our one God: Father, Son, and Holy Spirit. The icon reveals the unity between the three as an overflow of love. Each person is turned outward—toward one another—in selflessness, not inward, selfish or self-seeking. Jim Forest describes this icon in his book *Praying with Icons,* saying, "The Holy Trinity itself is a community of love so perfect that Father, Son and Holy Spirit are one. All creation is a manifestation of God's love."[2]

In the gospel of John, Christ prays for this overflow of love to affect those who believe in him. He prays that believers would be unified just as the Trinity models, "that they may be one as we are one—I in them and you in me—so that they may be brought to complete unity. Then the world will know that you sent me and have loved them even as you have loved me."[3]

God is a God of hospitality. He desires to make a home with us, within us. Christ revealed this in the Last Supper over wine and bread. And again, he made himself known at the supper at Emmaus. And in a passage at the end of the gospel of John that I have read over many times without it registering, Christ appears to the disciples again, this time after they have spent the morning fishing. He calls to them from the shore, "Did you catch anything?" "No," they answer, not knowing it is him. He instructs them to throw their net on the right side of the boat, and when they do, it is overflowing, just like the first day he called them to follow him. Now that they realize it is Christ on the shore, he again calls out, "Come and have breakfast," as he has started a fire to cook the fish.

God has revealed himself time and time again at the

table. At the table with Abraham and Sarah. At the Passover meal, when the Israelites had to prepare and eat their meals quickly. In the Last Supper, which we re-create at our churches each month or week or day. And at our own tables with our friends and family.

We talk about past meals we've devoured—the ones that elevated eating to another level, beyond simply fuel—because we long for the ultimate meal, the marriage supper of the Lamb, where we will all eat together as guests of Christ. When we will know and be known.

This is why we linger at the table. We strongly sense the *imago Dei*, the image of God, in each other at the table. Just as Christ's true self was uncovered at the table, at mealtimes we get a taste of the eternal—who we truly are and who we will be—and we long for it.

A few years ago, in Tuscany, we had the meal of a lifetime. My husband and I and our two sons traveled through Italy on sabbatical, two months off work provided by my husband's employer. My husband had read about Dario Cecchini, known as the world's most famous butcher.

Butchers from all over the world come to learn from Cecchini. His philosophy is to honor the animal from birth to death, and not one part of the beast, from head to tail, is wasted. Cecchini takes the happiness he remembers from eating around a big table with his family as a child and attempts to transport it to his restaurant. "I try and take a crumb of the joy from my childhood and bring it to the restaurant," he says. "I want everyone who comes to the butcher shop to think it's a day of celebration."[4]

After reading about Cecchini and his spirit, my husband knew he must experience a meal like this. The dining area is above the butcher shop. When we arrived during the middle of the day, it was as if we had walked into a party. People were spilling out of the butcher shop into the cobblestone street outside. They were laughing while drinking small glasses of red wine and nibbling on pieces of crusty farm bread with what I'd later learn was lardo, creamy raw pig fat whipped until it spreads like cream cheese. It is as decadent as it sounds.

A group of about forty of us had reservations for the next seating and were ushered upstairs into a long rectangular room with a large table along one side and ovens and grills for cooking meat along the other. Cecchini says, "Hospitality is sacred,"[5] and he sets the stage for a hallowed meal, reciting parts of Dante's *Divine Comedy* from memory as an invocation.

The diners watched as gigantic slabs of meat were brought in to cook. There was no seasoning but salt and pepper. Cecchini believes how the animal lived, from the food they ate to the environment they lived in, flavors the meat. And every course was meat.

Panning around the room, I saw and heard people from all walks of life and overheard at least five languages, from Italian, of course, to Chinese, German, Spanish, and my English. Throughout the meal, wine flowed and friends and neighbors shared bites and passed around each course as if we were now family. Each course was brought out to terrific fanfare as the chef joyously held the meat up in the air to announce its presence before slicing it. The entire table joined in a joyful chorus, cheering and clapping.

My sons were the only children at that table. My youngest was eight and delighted with everything. The chef enjoyed indulging him with the largest cuts of meat, including the *pièce de résistance,* the Florentine steak with the bone still in. My oldest son had the best seat at the table, directly next to the carving station where the chef cut each course, but he was more interested in rereading his favorite book at the time, *A Tree Grows in Brooklyn.* No one rolled their eyes at him or pressured him to eat more or participate more in the pageantry. He was accepted and appreciated just as he was, sitting and reading as he ate, just as he might have at home.

Even then, as I sat at that table eating with my family and with strangers, I thought, "This is what it will be like in heaven with Jesus." Strangers will become friends, brothers and sisters. People from many different backgrounds and with many different stories who are beloved by God will join at the table. Jesus will restore us to each other and to himself. He will fill us all with himself. And we will celebrate. What a joyous ruckus it will be!

25

of musical theater

Recently I heard a podcast where the guest said he wasn't a religious person, but the closest he had experienced to the transcendent was musical theater. Life "set to music, including its regularities and harmonies and probably culminating in people, all doing things together, partly in rhythm and singing in big harmony," he reflected to the host. "It seems to give life a kind of a transcendental meaning, and to me, that sounds like, feels like church."[1] My ears perked up when I heard this because it is not an overstatement to say musical theater changed my life.

Yes, I was a high school theater kid. Musical theater condensed many life lessons into one spring rehearsal schedule. My first show was *How to Succeed in Business Without Really Trying*. This was before the Harry Potter kid played the lead in a revival on Broadway. This was back when it was still a sleepy old 1960s musical no one had ever heard of. The original lead on Broadway, Robert Morse, would go on play

Bertram Cooper on AMC's *Mad Men*, which in many ways was an homage to this musical.

When my high school theater program performed *How to Succeed*, no one knew the songs or was familiar with its mid-century mod style. It was mildly sexist, and we knew it. Most of the songs that feature this sexism have since been scrubbed from the roster. In some ways, it is a shame, for it was in those songs that we young women learned to play. We learned the power and protection needed in our sexuality. And in that setting, I learned to laugh and love more than any other time in my life.

For three months we lived and breathed this musical. We sang its songs between classes and practiced the dance steps at lunch. We hung out with the same thirty people from the cast and crew not only at rehearsals but also at meals and on rides and late nights when we were too amped to go to sleep.

In that group of kids, we learned how to deal with conflict. We learned that differences in our abilities, backgrounds, and views on life were to be cherished. We learned to work as a team.

Most of us, like myself, were only moderately talented. We had to work hard to hit the notes, find the harmonies, keep up with the steps. But a few of us were actual talents—the type of presence and voice and grace that would go on to elite music and acting programs, including our lead, who went to Juilliard and then performed Shakespeare professionally.

We knew who those kids were. That they were marked, golden, gifted. But the thing is, we felt honored to lift them up. We supported them, never in jealousy but in pride. We were honored to be part of their story in some way.

I don't think I am idealistic in saying that. I could talk to any of those kids today because I still know most of them. We were knitted together in such a way in those three months that we could pick up any other day, any other year, and each of them would say we were our best selves during that time together.

We were plural. True community. We learned to love and protect each other, fiercely.

But it was the music that stirred our souls. We lifted our voices in silliness and humor but also in longing for love and understanding, a desire to be known. The music articulated these dreams in a way that made them appropriate to express aloud. We sang these songs riotously, at the top of our voices, with our eyes closed, in front of the boy we had a crush on, in front of the girl we hated, in front of our parents, in the middle of the small quad in front of the much more popular or beautiful people, because we could. It was theater.

The first time a song from a musical moved me in such a way was during my family's annual viewing of *The Wizard of Oz*. It is incomprehensible to many now, but there was a time when *The Wizard of Oz* was shown only once a year on television. This was before VCRs and DVDs and cable and streaming. When CBS broadcasted the annual showing of *Oz*, it was an *event*. This was true not only in my home but in others' too. If someone had a larger television than most, they might host a party. A friend of mine said it was the only night of the year they were allowed Cheese Whiz, a luxury item for a lower middle class elementary-aged child in the 1980s. Others tell me their family wore costumes.

In my family we were not allowed much television. Perhaps a weekly episode of *Little House on the Prairie* before it was syndicated, but that was pretty much it. *Wizard of Oz* night was one of the only nights a year my sisters and I were allowed to stay up well past our bedtimes. With commercial breaks, the film took well over three hours. We'd take our nightly baths early that evening and eat our dinner in our pajamas before the glow of our thirteen-inch television set.

When Judy Garland sang "Over the Rainbow," I sat enrapt. She seemed to be a little girl still, not much older than us. I couldn't understand how she could make her voice sound like that. The longing and purity in her voice made me want to cry for reasons I did not yet understand.

It was years before we got a color television and I learned that everything turns to color when Dorothy lands in Oz. My sisters and I *gasped aloud* when Dorothy opened her front door to step into a technicolor dream. We didn't know the blue of her dress, the golden rod of the yellow brick road, or the fanciful colors of the Munchkins' clothes. It was as if we were seeing the film for the first time.

This was also the moment in the film when we'd take turns on my mother's lap as she carefully combed out our hair, braided and twisted it into "Dorothy hair." She spun pink foam rollers on the end of each braid so we'd wake in the morning with perfect round curls, just like Judy Garland.

My mother, sisters, and I would belt out each song with the film, sometimes standing up to dance. It was an interactive experience, one we planned and looked forward to on the family calendar.

Back in theater class, before we were dating, my future husband, Justo, made an announcement. The incomparable Mandy Patinkin would be performing as Uncle Archibald in the new *The Secret Garden* musical. Patinkin was already a theater legend at this time. The musical was sold out in Los Angeles where we lived, but there were still tickets in San Diego, a two-hour drive away. Justo had a 1972 Chevy Malibu with bench seats, which we had already learned could seat around eight or nine of us theater kids in a pinch. He offered to drive anyone who wanted to go.

I didn't know Justo very well at that time. All I knew was that he was intimidating. He was huge—six-foot, two inches—and wore what we called monkey boots, large sturdy boots with ten sets of holes for laces. Anyone who wore boots like that must have seen things. And I had once seen him play Othello in a Shakespeare competition. When he killed Desdemona, I thought he really did, even though Desdemona was played by my friend Jen, who was my ride home from the competition. He had a *presence.*

But I had also heard he'd read a girl Dylan Thomas poems on a date. That was surprising to me.

I saved up and bought a ticket to the musical along with another girl from our class named Mizuha. The three of us laughed that we were quite a trio: the huge Mexican with a leather jacket and boots, me, a tall translucent girl wearing some sort of gunny sack excuse for a dress, and a small Japanese girl in her preppy best.

I'm fairly certain he would say I must be mistaken, but

I remember looking over at Justo during Mandy Patinkin and Robert Westenberg's number "Lily's Eyes," where two brothers sing of their love for the now-deceased Lily, to find his eyes moist—wet, maybe even brimming. The Dylan Thomas rumor came to mind, and I no longer found him intimidating but intriguing. We would not date until a good decade later, but *The Secret Garden* revealed a new layer to this complicated man.

Daisy Eagan was only eleven years old when she won the Tony for her performance as Mary Lennox in that run of *The Secret Garden*. Over twenty-five years later, Justo and I would take our own sons to their first musical theater performance, a revival of *The Secret Garden* with Eagan now playing the maid, Martha. Our hope was that they, too, would fall in love with musical theater, and they did.

A few years ago, when I took my oldest son to a performance of *Dear Evan Hansen*, he was the only dry eye in the house when the cast performed "You Will Be Found." It occurred to me that this was because he hadn't felt lost yet. When I looked around at us—teenagers, middle-aged moms, and old hippies—I understood how this experience could be church to someone. The audience sang along, with tears streaming down their faces about their hope that "when the dark comes crashing through . . . someone will come running to take you home."

For me, and perhaps for others in the audience, the song wasn't my hope for the future but a reminiscence of the times in my life when God's grace shone through and saved me. Often from myself. I can't help but think of the song as a hymn, similar to "Amazing Grace" or "How Great Thou Art."

The song also speaks of the image of God within us. It says we are valuable, something to save, and that we have the ability to be God's hands and feet when someone we love is suffering.

To experience all these emotions, whether consciously or unconsciously, as part of a mass of people did feel transcendent. *Dear Evan Hansen* reflected part of our stories up on that stage, shared in a way we couldn't: our plea to know we are not alone.

Last week I was in charge of carpool. I loaded my car with my teen sons and their friends to drive them to the next extracurricular activity. They were loud and giggly—something about a rumor at school so ridiculously untrue that it bore repeating. But when the song "Waving Through a Window" from *Dear Evan Hansen* came on the stereo, all chatter slowed down. "Quiet!" one said. "Shhhh," said another. "I know, I love this song." And then full-bodied and voiced, they began to sing along. The girl in the front seat rolled down her window and let her hand glide in the wind. A boy in the back closed his eyes. They sang in one voice about the fears and anxieties of the teen years, without guile or self-consciousness. They sang of their desire to be known—right in front of me. I could do nothing but join them.

26

of the urban bestiary

She walks through the yard like she owns the place, but I don't know her. And this is *my yard*! She sashays down our paved walkway, looking to the left, then to the right as if she's deciding whether she likes what we've done to the landscaping.

Then she looks straight at me. She knows I am watching from the window. Without breaking eye contact, she slinks under our deck until all I can see is her furry, practically coiffed tail.

The nerve!

I don't think she is a stray. She's too judgmental, posh, well kept, and I can tell she has a brutal side. She will cut you if she doesn't like the way you look at her.

A rabbit bolts out from the other end of the deck. Posh Spice darts out right after him. He's gone though. He's found another place to hide, and she looks back at me as if to say, "You gotta problem?"

Nope. I'm just enjoying watching the drama unfold. And I'm allergic to cats.

It's not only cats I see in my yard. I practically have a menagerie, not that I noticed until, like most, the pandemic lockdowns had me *scheduling* "window time" each day.

I've always been a city girl. I grew up in Los Angeles and moved to Seattle nearly eighteen years ago. I have always lived close to a downtown area. In Los Angeles, on days when there was no smog, I could see the downtown skyscrapers from the end of my block, and now from my home in Seattle, I can see downtown from one window on the second floor during the winter, when there are no leaves on the tree outside.

When my husband and I first moved to Seattle, we enthusiastically watched the birds that flock to our yard. Because we grew up with mostly pigeons or seagulls, even a house finch thrilled us.

We were surprised to discover hummingbirds stopping in for a sip of nectar from our flowers. Flocks of starlings landed in our yard to search for bugs and then left *en masse* without notice. We even saw a bald eagle now and then, soaring high above Lake Washington, located not far from our home. Yet the most interesting discovery was the never-ending drama between the crows and the American robin couple guarding their new nest.

My husband hollered into the house from his yardwork, "It's back on!" as if it were a soap opera on television. I took two cups of coffee out to the deck, and we watched the story unfold. Up to this point, the robin couple had been able to defend their nest. But that day, the crows ganged up on them, separating them, leaving the nest unguarded. A crow swooped in, stealing an egg and *dramatically eating it* atop our neighbor's roof. The robins squawked loudly on the telephone wires overhead.

"It sounds like crying," I said with tears in my eyes.

My husband, more pragmatic said, "That's why they're called a murder of crows," grabbing his shears and returning to work.

I stayed, sipping my coffee when the phrase "Are not you more important than they?" popped into my head. I knew exactly where it was from: Jesus's Sermon on the Mount, when he talked about dependence on God: "Look at the birds of the air; they do not sow or reap or store away in barns, and yet your heavenly Father feeds them. Are you not much more valuable than they? Can any one of you by worrying add a single hour to your life?"[1] A biblical life lesson played out in dramatic fashion in an afternoon in my yard.

In the first few months of the pandemic, everyone in my neighborhood began noticing the rabbits. We hadn't had them before. Or at least not enough to notice. Then all of a sudden, they were *everywhere*. It was a little COVID gift. We all needed something cute and cheerful to watch from our decks and windows, and Seattle is perfect for rabbits. There is always something lush and green to eat, and our winters are so mild, these cottontails can make it through the cold months.

My friend, writer and naturalist Lyanda Lynn Haupt, says in her delightful book *The Urban Bestiary*, "The rural buffer that once separated cities from wilderness in the past is disappearing."[2] This is part of the reason I am seeing more and more animals in my yard, on my block, and in my neighborhood. My neighbor who has been in the neighborhood decades longer than me said she used to see foxes on our street. I have never seen one, but I am seeing more animals. Our neighborhood butts up against seventeen acres of forest. Yep, right in the middle of the city, a pocket of forest. Neighborhoods envelop this forest on each side, and at night the creatures of the forest creep out to see what we have left behind. Lyanda says, "Wild animals are left with smaller, more fragmented areas in which to live, eat and breed."[3] Like my postage stamp of a yard.

Of course there are also squirrels in my yard, but Keanu is my favorite. Yes, we named him Keanu. I am not certain who named him, but we say his name so matter-of-factly now. "Keanu's having a playdate with his friend, the plastic bag, again!" someone will holler from their viewing spot at their window. Each of us will stop what we are doing to run to a window and watch Keanu. Sure enough, there he is, practically dancing with that plastic bag, trash untethered from its can. Keanu dashes the bag into the air, runs ahead of it, catches his paw in the edge, waving it back and forth like some sort of Gene Kelly dream sequence. "He loves that bag," I hear one of my sons say dryly from his perch.

Not all the animals delight us. Last autumn a pack of raccoons visited our yard at night. They were looking for grubs to eat. In the morning, our green grass had been turned into a pile of earth. The raccoons had peeled the grass back with their nails and then dug into the soil. Each morning greeted us with what looked like a freshly dug grave.

We placed motion detectors that shone a bright light on

the masked critters, as if they were trying to break out of prison, but the raccoons only thanked us for the well-lit area to dig in. We found motion detectors that emitted a high-pitched screech heard only by critters. They simply knocked them over.

My husband decided to take matters into his own hands. He stayed up well past bedtime to sit outside in the dark with a BB gun in his hands and a cigar lit in his mouth. (He had to pass the time!) He looked like General George S. Patton out there waiting for the enemy to strike. He did manage to dislocate a few tufts of fur but nothing serious—nothing to deter the creatures.

When our yard finally looked like a construction zone, we hired men to churn the earth, give us *fresh* dirt, resoil, and resod. It was costly, and honestly I am not certain how permanent this solution is, but my husband is smoking less and sleeping more.

Yes, coming this close to nature without leaving my house is annoying, but it is also thrilling. I've noticed we are on one opossum's circuit. He doesn't come often, maybe once a month, just to see if we are interesting. He stays close to the fence, watching us from afar as he crawls along the perimeter. My husband makes unkind jokes about a well-known actress, and I pretend not to hear him.

On early morning runs, I see the outline of coyotes a block or two ahead of me. I can tell they're not just stray dogs, for there might be two or three of them, running together with that straight-legged run of theirs. Seeing them puts a damper on my run. I feel I need to stay on guard, although attacks on humans are rare and usually involve the human trying to feed them, which I am not stupid enough to do. Yet seeing these wild animals has another effect on me: It makes me feel more human. The disparity between them and me makes me hyperaware of my *humanness*, especially my ability to contain and control emotion. I think about this for a mile or so until I am so incredibly grateful for the disparity and for the gift of being able to see these creatures.

Thirteen years ago, while pregnant with my youngest son, I couldn't sleep. I put on a kettle for tea and looked out onto the deck at three o'clock in the morning to find a bobcat curled up by our glass doors. It took me a while to realize what I was looking at. It was certainly larger than a cat and had those unmistakable pointed bobcat ears. I held my breath as I watched it and it watched me. The encounter became something of a fable or myth I blamed on insomnia or pregnancy delusions.

My bobcat story became intertwined with the stories of my pregnancy until last week, when I left early to drive to the gym. It was still dark out. I found two rabbits, frozen in motion, by my car. I found that odd. They usually scamper when I approach. I said good morning to them, but they did not budge. It was as if they were paralyzed. I followed their line of sight, and there he was, perched atop the fence, looking down at us: a bobcat. I too froze, blinked. And then he was gone.

I scrambled quickly into the car, unsure if I was still asleep or awake. I looked back, and there he was at the end of the sidewalk, his eyes flashing red in the darkness.

Each of these encounters jars me out of complacency, reminding me that I am not alone in this world. That while I sleep, life continues outside the walls of my home. This world is not just about me. I am sharing it with all of creation. Even a city girl like me, especially a city girl like me, needs to be reminded of this.

27

in the darkest of places

The light was dim. Most of the windows were broken, stuffed with rags to keep out the cold. The two sisters knew the place was revolting even before their eyes became accustomed to the dark. The stench of soiled and rancid linens hung in the air. As they were pushed through the room single-file, they saw the makeshift beds were platforms three levels high, rising nearly to the ceiling, giving the narrow aisles and the beds an extremely claustrophobic condition. These middle-aged sisters were directed to climb into a middle platform covered with reeking, urine-damp straw.

The location was Ravensbrück, a concentration camp for women in Hitler's Germany. The two Ten Boom sisters were Christians from the Netherlands confined for the crime of hiding and rescuing Jews from destruction and death. Corrie cried out to her sister, "How can we live in such a place?"

Betsie replied, "Show us how."

It took her stunned sister a moment to realize Betsie was praying: "The distinction between prayer and the rest of life seemed to be vanishing for Betsie."[1]

Betsie animatedly reminded her sister of the Scripture they had read that very morning in the Bible they had smuggled into the camp: "Rejoice always, pray constantly, give thanks in all circumstances."[2] This seemed a tall order considering the surroundings, but Betsie was determined. "We can start right now to thank God for every single thing about this new barracks!"

Corrie was less enthusiastic, but Betsie showed her the way. She gave thanks that they were placed together and had each other. They had not been searched, they still retained their Bible, and with such cramped quarters, more women would hear and be comforted by God's Word. They even thanked God for the fleas that had begun to gnaw on their bodies during these prayers.

A concentration camp seems a most unlikely place to exude joy. But then I think, "Isn't that sort of condition when joy is truly 'light in the darkness'?" Happiness is tied to our human experience, when life is going the way we planned. Joy is something altogether different. Joy is tied to something deeper, something otherworldly.

Betsie was so deeply connected to God that her life and prayer life had no distinction. She had entered into that space Saint Paul calls us to: praying without ceasing.[3] It was this practice of surrender that allowed her to open herself to joy in the most wretched of places.

Later, Betsie and Corrie learn why they and the other women in their quarters experienced relatively more "freedom" than those in the other barracks. They retained their Bible, held religious services, and received fewer brutal beatings—all because of the fleas. Betsie overheard the guards confessing why they rarely entered the quarters: for fear of being eaten alive. Betsie could only laugh as she shared this with her sister.

This story is painful to read, but it gives me hope. These sisters had a faith so strong, so instilled in their being, that even in the darkest of places the sisters could still look for gratitude, for laughter, for hope, and for joy. This is the faith I desire.

Real faith isn't present only when it is utilitarian, when it is convenient. True faith is part of you, how you live and move and have your being.

True faith is when Job loses everything yet does not deny God. Job stood resolute in his faith even when his closest friends tried to sway him to curse God. True faith is how Betsie's two worlds, the seen and unseen, began to merge. It is how she was able to see God moving in the darkest of places. When you practice joy, joy is the default, even when the world falls apart.

After the terrorist group Hamas butchered over 1,200 Jews in Israel on October 7, 2023, my friend, an Israeli, wandered the streets in grief. He was snapped out of his trance by the shouts of a man marching down Gaza Ave. waving an Israeli flag. The man marched past Netanyahu's private apartment, his tzitzit flying in the wind, shouting above the traffic, *"Simhah lehiyot besimhah"* (Joy, be joyful.) True joy still thrives when you are bent, pressed, and straightened. This man's act was one of defiance, and it reminded my friend to do the same.

My Jewish friend tells me this is his faith at its best. "This is what we have been taught since the beginning of time." During the Babylonian exile God told the Israelites to "build houses and settle down; plant gardens and eat what they produce. Marry and have sons and daughters; find wives for your sons and give your daughters in marriage, so that they too may have sons and daughters. Increase in number there; do not decrease. Also, seek the peace and prosperity of the city to which I have carried you into exile."[4]

With faith in God, we will not despair. Even in the darkest of places, we will create, build, plant, love, and hope.

Paul's letter to the Romans was written to a group of mostly Jewish converts to Christianity who, like Jews generations before them, had experienced years of exile from their homes. Emperor Claudius had them expelled from Rome years before. These Romans to whom Paul wrote had just returned to their homes now that Claudius had died. They were discouraged, dejected, and dispirited. Paul echoes a bit of those words from the prophets centuries before: There is "glory in our sufferings, because we know that suffering produces perseverance; perseverance, character; and character, hope. And hope does not put us to shame."[5] Hope does not disappoint.

We often forget the crux of our faith, nay, the cross of our faith: that there was—*is*—redemption in our Savior's suffering. And he suffered to join in our own suffering. It is often in the midst of the deepest of suffering that we are able to know Christ in the most tangible way. Our faith is a paradox, to the world and often to ourselves.

28

in silence

It was a three-hour drive. Alone.

Usually on long solo car drives, I listen to music or catch up on phone calls or podcasts, but this time I decided to drive in silence.

It seemed a wise thing to do, but also a little wacky. I was on my way to a weekend silent retreat. I try to do this at least once a year to reset myself. To get rid of the noise—not only of my environment but also in my mind and spirit.

A friend offered their home on the Washington coast, three hours from Seattle, as a refuge while they were out of town. I figured I might as well use those three hours to start early, to prepare for my weekend of silence. But I was on my way to a weekend of silence! Wouldn't I get all the silence I needed later? How about one last hurrah of noise?

I have to admit, I started talking to myself. I felt like that guy in the film *Fargo*—you know, the funny looking one? He can't stand it that his co-criminal will not chat as he drives the long journey from Fargo, North Dakota, to Minneapolis,

Minnesota. He keeps repeating, "I don't have to talk either, man! See how you like it. Just total . . . silence. Two can play at that game, smart guy." Except it was me talking. To myself.

I read signs aloud. I counted down the minutes, miles to my destination. I rewarded myself every quarter of an hour with a rousing rendition of old folk songs my mother played when I was a child.

And then I remembered Pascal's quote: "Man's unhappiness springs from one thing alone, his incapacity to stay quietly in one room."[1] I think he would say the same about a car.

Wasn't this the entire premise of the weekend? To learn how to be silent? To "be still, and know that [he is] God"?[2]

I took a deep breath and listened. My head was full of noise: fragments from music I usually have on in the background, a social media post that annoyed me a day ago, a bit of a commercial from twenty years ago, and the phantom buzz of my phone's notifications. Yes, this is why I was taking this weekend in silence; it was a racket in there.

When I was a child, my home life was never calm. There was a lot of yelling and tension and the general feeling that someone was going to do the wrong thing at any moment—and that that person might be me. In high school, every once in a while, my future husband, Justo, would call me on a Saturday and ask if I wanted to go for a drive. He worked for his family's auto repair business, and occasionally his father would ask him to go pick up a part in the Valley. It takes a long time to get there and back. Justo and I weren't particularly close or even friends, but I now understand he sensed I wouldn't mind getting out of the house.

The drive took hours, and the two of us would rarely talk. We listened to The Clash, The Drifters, and Louis Prima, all music that seemed to take us to another time. Although the car wasn't silent for the music, there was a kind of silence. I didn't need to entertain my classmate or make him feel secure or better about himself. We could just be. It was a gift. I returned to my house refreshed. I had the space to breathe, to not feel tension or worry.

Thirteen years later I would marry him. Those car rides were an indicator and foretaste of why I would fall in love with him. His silence gave me the space to breathe and grow and become the person I was created to be.

Isn't that what God wants to do? And now on my way to the retreat, here he was, offering himself in a weekend of silence. He always is. Wouldn't I be a fool not to sit in it?

Cardinal Robert Sarah says, "Sounds and emotions detach us from ourselves, whereas silence always forces man to reflect upon his own life."[3] I see this in my own life. The notifications, the connection to my phone, the general brain clutter—it all distracts me from me, and ultimately from God. So I stop reading the signs on the road, I stop counting the miles and minutes, and simply drive in silence with God.

"For God alone my soul waits in silence."[4] If I push through the discomfort and, frankly, the minutiae of silence, something always happens: actual silence. The noise stops. The tape on repeat in my head stops playing. And suddenly I am *present*. I am in the moment before me, and I can *see*. The road is no longer about signs and mile markers but about the scenery around me: geese landing in a pond off the highway, wind in the trees, and waterways ribboning through the landscape. It's not just that I am present; it's that God is present—and I am noticing. All that noise is gone, and he is filling it with himself. The still, small voice we often find difficult to hear is near. What I once thought was a little pocket of his presence, in the back seat or glove box of the car, expands until it fills the space. Goodness and peace fill the car and my mind, and I realize how distracted I have been with silliness that keeps me from who he created me to be.

Again, it is Cardinal Sarah's words I turn to: "Through silence, we return to our heavenly origin, where there is nothing but calm, peace, repose, silent contemplation, and adoration of the radiant face of God."[5] This is where silence leads you: toward worship. Because when you are faced with his presence, you realize how trite and silly your noise and problems and focus are and how wonderful—how full of awe, beauty, and goodness—he is. How everything is under his control. When you finally see the bigger picture God is trying to show, you see it all as a gift. In return, all you can do is praise.

You praise him for the geese and the trees and for creating you. For giving you a weekend away, the luxury of sitting in his presence.

I am grateful that I chose to drive in quiet. The time serves as a labyrinth in many ways, slowing me down, preparing me for the weekend ahead. When I arrive at my friend's home, I stay in silence. I hear the refrigerator turning on and then off and the wind in the crawl spaces and attic of the large old house. I hear the electricity buzzing in the wires and lamps, and I can hear God. Silence connects us back to our Creator.

There was a time, years ago, before my children were born, before my marriage, when I was afraid of silence. I knew God was on the other side.

I knew I had made horrible choices and done horrible things, that word that even Christians no longer want to say: *sin*.

I was soaked in sin. I took one step in that direction, and the next step was so easy, until I was walking in deep, thick, sticky sin.

Everyone around me could smell it. Holy people reached out their hands to me. "Oh no!" they cried. "Let me help pull you out!" I certainly did not want to bring this filth to God. I didn't want to talk about what I'd been up to. Other people wanted to help me too. These were the people who wanted to show me the quicksand. I sunk and watched the sticky sin rise around me. It stuck to me. I was stuck. I would never be clean. I would never get out.

These moments are like a Flannery O'Connor story come to life. In her stories it is always at the grossest, dirtiest, most embarrassing, awkward, sticky sin–filled moment of the character's lives that God offers them grace. Grace was always there, but perhaps we can't see it until we are at our worst. And it is often a moment when we were nowhere near looking for God because, we find, he was pursuing us as we ran away from him.

Nineteenth-century Catholic poet Francis Thompson knew this moment too. He wrote of it in his poem "The Hound of Heaven." Like me, Thompson "fled Him, down the nights and down the days / [he] fled Him, down the arches of the years." Looking back, I can see it now too—how

God was right there after me. Maybe I was frightened of him. Perhaps this is why I kept moving further and deeper into the quicksand, as Thompson did, running

> From those strong Feet that followed, followed after.
> But with unhurrying chase,
> And unperturbed pace,
> Deliberate speed, majestic instancy
> They beat . . .[6]

I was afraid of the silence, of surrendering, and as Thompson puts it, "I knew His love Who followed." But I was afraid of his love.

In our mind, a God who waits for you to love him is much easier. That's a tidy god, a god who waits at the church building for you. Much more difficult to comprehend is a God who pursues you through the mud and the mire at an "unhurrying chase," with majesty snapping birch branches along the path to reach out to you in the muck. A God who wants to love you even when you don't want him to, even with you are filthy and he must moisten his hands with spit to wipe away the dirt from your eyes so you can see that he's standing right in front of you—that's a frightening God. That's the God who goes after the one lost lamb, especially when that lamb is you.

The silence we were so afraid of is rest. It means being held in the arms of the One who loves us most. The One who loves us enough to let us grab onto him when we are filthy and sticky and soiled. The One who pulls us up out of the mire.

And we learn—I learned—he isn't scary at all. It's the kind of silence that led me to fall in love with my husband. The kind of silence that generates shelter, a space to breathe and grow and become the person our Creator created us to be.

29

# of coffee

Black. Commuter mug. *Good coffee needs nothing added.*

Keurig. Vanilla coffee creamer. Favorite rainbow mug from 1993.

French press. Skim milk. Sugar. China teacup and saucer.

Does coffee even know how much it means to us?

Some nights when I go to bed, I lie there and think about how good my coffee is going to taste in the morning. Yes, I fall asleep with visions of coffee cups dancing in my head.

I was in fifth grade when I first started drinking coffee. Yes, I agree it was too early, but can you just listen to my story first?

Back then we lived in a little alley in East LA (unincorporated Montebello, if you want to get technical), across the street from my mom's mom, my nana. It was the same alley my mother had grown up on. Everyone knew us, and we knew everyone.

Each morning, I'd finish getting ready for school before everyone else in my house. I had to get up early to make sure my bangs were perfectly teased into a faux waterfall and then sprayed with Aqua Net until they were impenetrable. I needed the bathroom to myself for that business. So I woke up early. While the rest of the family got dressed and had their breakfast, I walked across the street to have coffee with my nana and watch *Good Morning America*.

She drew open the drapes on the big picture window in front of her house to let me know she was awake and left the screen door unlocked. Nana sat at her dining room table, her back to the television in the den on low. As soon as I walked into her house, I smelled the coffee in the percolator and her cigarette smoke, as I usually caught her first drag of the day.

I had heard coffee stunted your growth. At eleven years old, I was already five foot six, towering over the mostly Mexican boys in my class. My mother was nearly six feet tall. At this rate I'd surpass her height even without my magnificent bangs. Coffee seemed a perfect solution.

General Foods International Coffees had recently come out with flavors that promised to import you to Europe in a single cup. I now think that was because they are pure sugar. You were so incredibly hyped on sugar and caffeine that you thought you were sitting on a canal in Venice as a gondolier glided by. I mixed two tablespoons into a mug of coffee from the percolator, sat at the large oak table with Nana, and listened to Charles Gibson tell us what was going on in the world. I felt very sophisticated.

And, you know, I think it worked. I'm only five foot nine.

Nespresso. Room for cream. Sugar in the Raw.

Mr. Coffee. Skim milk. Splenda.

Pour over. Like mud.

There are mornings when coffee may be the sole reason we get up.

I feel horrible. I might be coming down with a cold or nuclear war . . . but coffee might make it all more manageable.

There is something about being able to participate in the ritual of morning coffee, whatever that is for you. Whether it is making coffee just for yourself or for a loved one too. In my home, only my husband knows the perfect coffee-sugar-milk ratio I take. Even I do not know. Some days I think that ratio might be the secret to the entire universe.

It might be the most present we are in the entire day as we inhale the scent of the cup, close our eyes, and take a sip, establishing the true beginning of the day. Nothing tastes as good as that first sip. Not the second sip. Not the first sip from your third cup. It is that *first* sip. It fortifies us.

I know some people don't drink coffee. I myself drink tea when I go to the UK. (When in Rome!) But we aren't talking about them. We are talking about the nearly 80 percent of Americans who drink coffee. You see, it is one of the things most of us have in common. We might differ on politics or religion or whether we eat carbs, but *do you need a cup o' joe to function in the morning? So do I!* Through coffee we see our shared humanity. I too am a walking sack of bones and flesh until I have a morning jolt of caffeine to jump-start my heart and brain.

But truly, honestly, there are days when my coffee feels like grace. My heart is already racing with the day before me. And I want to sob, I am so overwhelmed. I warm my hands on the mug, close my eyes, and breathe. Just breathe. In that space between my own breath and the steam from the cup,

I know God is there. "He is not far from any one of us."[1] In that moment, I am aware of the Holy Spirit within me and the presence of grace.

My cup and portion. My cup overflows. Cup of mercy. Goodness.

That cup of coffee is a prayer. A moment when we ask for what we have not words for. The moment of "Be still, and know I am God." And in that breath, in acknowledging Your presence, You show us You will make a way where we see none.

30

of books

I cheated on my kindergarten entry exam.

My mother had taken me to see the campus and meet the principal. After the tour there was a test that included a few flash cards of shapes—a circle, square, and the elusive rectangle—and, for some reason, showing the principal how I held a pencil in my hand.

Then he brought out crayons. He asked me to tell him what color they were: green, brown, red, blue. Right there on the side of the blue crayon I saw it said *sky blue*. I didn't even think about it. Instead of saying "light blue" as he probably wanted, expected, I said, "Sky blue." As soon as the words left my mouth, I realized what I had done. I had probably ruined it all. I was sure they didn't let cheater children like me into the school. It was a Christian school after all. They had standards! My mother couldn't afford this school. I knew someone else was going to pay. And, well, now I blew it because I was a cheater.

All the energy left the principal's office. I put my head

down in shame but waited until we got into my mother's seaweed-green Ford Pinto to spill the beans.

"I cheated!" I blurted out once she closed the driver's side door.

"What do you mean you cheated?"

"I read the name of the color off the side of the crayon—sky blue!" I tried not to cry.

My mother began to laugh. I didn't understand how she could find this so funny. "You read the name of the color? That's not cheating. You can read, and now your principal knows that too."

I hadn't thought of it that way. I had learned to read through hours of *Sesame Street* and visits from my grandmother, who worked as a teacher's aide. She brought *Dick and Jane* books and lined paper for me to learn to write my letters on when she visited.

I ended up getting into the school after all. And on the first day of kindergarten, I brought a book—you know, just in case I got bored. I suppose that is when it all started. I always have a book under my arm or in my purse or under the passenger seat in my car in case of an emergency.

One of my earliest memories of reading is from my first few years of elementary school. The house we rented in Pico Rivera, California, was small and busy. We had the honor of having my great-grandmother live with us during that time, and my mother watched other children besides my two sisters and me. The house could be loud and chaotic. Yet I found the perfect spot for reading: a hall closet with an accordion door with slats that let in the perfect amount of light to read by. I slipped inside; sat crisscross on my great-grandmother's old hope chest, which lay perfectly between two shelves of board games; and pulled the door back, flush. No one knew I was inside. There I read *Ramona* books and became lost—absolutely lost—among *Monopoly, Sorry,* and *The Ungame* until I heard someone call my name and bring me out of my reverie.

Ramona was constantly confused about the world around her, and so was I. In *Ramona the Pest,* Ramona's teacher told her to sit in a chair for the present. Ramona sat and wondered what the present would be, only to find out the teacher meant for the present time, as in sit there for right now. I understood exactly what Ramona was going through! And I felt like Ramona would understand me. She would have understood how confused I was when my father was watching the news and I heard there were gorillas fighting in the jungles of Nicaragua. Of course, I was reading a book when I heard this. I kept peeking over the spine of my book hoping to catch a glimpse of these gorillas on the television screen. My father noticed my big, worried eyes and finally asked me what was wrong. "How did the gorillas get the guns?" I asked.

Ramona wouldn't have laughed at me.

By the time third grade came along, most of my friends were characters in books: Laura and Mary from the *Little House on the Prairie* books, Nancy Drew, and Charlie from *Charlie and the Chocolate Factory.* My teacher noticed this about me. She noticed I didn't really connect with the other girls in class who were already talking about boys and breaking into different factions each recess. One day after school, she gave me a book with a redheaded girl like me on the cover and said, "Since you like to read, I thought you would enjoy reading this book. You remind me of her," she said, pointing to the cover. The book was *Anne of Green Gables*, and I read it all that night before I went to sleep.

I felt like Anne in ways I couldn't yet articulate, but the book gave me language for what I was feeling and how I moved through the world. I couldn't believe my teacher saw this in me. It was a jarring notion. I felt both honored and seen, but if she could see it, who else could? I had begun to cherish my inner life. As with Anne, it was a place where I could go and hide, but if my teacher could see this, would others? Would they try to take it away from me?

I quickly learned that not everyone cares enough to notice. And in Anne, I too found my "kindred spirit." She was described as a "no commonplace soul," and her "body might be there at the table, but her spirit was far way in some remote airy cloudland, borne aloft on the wings of imagination."[1] Anne was starved, unloved, and intense, characteristics I connected with in a home with too many children and not enough food or attention. Yet Anne, simply by being who she was, changed the people around her. Slowly her community saw through her eyes and learned to love. I wanted that.

For now, Anne would be my friend and teacher.

I learned to find these friends in books especially when I felt disconnected and misplaced. In books I never felt lonely, and I always found a friend.

I found the transcendentalists in high school. In Emerson and Thoreau, I discovered friends who encouraged my individualism and self-reliance. "Whoso would be a man, must be a nonconformist,"[2] Ralph whispered in my ear. Henry

David agreed: "If a man does not keep pace with his companions, perhaps it is because he hears a different drummer. Let him step to the music he hears, however measured or far away."[3] I learned to embrace who I was and who I was becoming.

In college at California State University, Long Beach, I saw myself in both Elinor and Marianne in *Sense and Sensibility*. Both Dashwood sisters were who I was and who I wanted to be. And in *Frankenstein*, I identified with the creature's longing for connection with his creator and his insatiable hunger to teach and know himself.

In seminary, after several grueling months of navel-gazing and immersing myself in theology texts, I felt spent and exhausted. A classmate noticed. "I was having a day like yours last week; this will help you feel better," she said, handing me a volume of Wendell Berry poetry. His poetry grounded me in a world outside the seminary building and outside myself where God's peace was available and preset in nature and the land. Even if I didn't have time to drive out to the country, I could find my own peace in "wild things" through his words.

By the time I read *Anna Karenina* by the pool in Palo Alto the summer I fell in love with my soon-to-be husband, I knew exactly who I was. I knew I didn't want the tragedy of Anna and Count Vronsky's affair. I wanted love that was solid, dependable, and drama free. I could never be friends with those characters, but I could use their experience as a cautionary tale.

Through these books and characters, I learned I need never be alone. In a book, there is always someone interesting to spend time with and to learn from. So I wasn't surprised one night after dinner to see my son curled up with *A Tree Grows in Brooklyn.* He has read it and reread it nearly fifty times now. My husband asked, "What's so great about that book? Isn't it just about a girl growing up in Brooklyn?" My son, dumbfounded, looked up from his book. "No, it is not just about a girl growing up in Brooklyn!" Then he proceeded to give us a thirty-minute lecture on the merits and insight of Francie Nolan. I knew then that my son had a friend in Francie Nolan. She understood his inner life better than the rest of us did.

31

# of travel

The first time I traveled by plane, I was twenty-five years old.

I'd grown up poor. We weren't the type of family who boarded a plane with rolling carry-ons or little donut pillows around our necks for vacations. We were the type of family that filled a duffle bag, or maybe even a plastic trash bag, with a hoodie and some extra pairs of underwear and socks, stuck an old tent in the back of the car, drove as far as we could in two hours, and set up camp. Sometimes that was even in a designated campsite!

I grew up in urban East Los Angeles, so even the suburbs were exciting for me. (All that land! You couldn't see directly into your neighbor's window!) Camping anywhere that even slightly resembled the country was glorious to me and my younger sisters. Once I woke in a cold sleeping bag to the sound of cows mooing on a hillside near where we were camping and thought I was practically Laura Ingalls

Wilder. I got teary-eyed because those beasts were beautiful and smelly and other-worldly.

Honestly, back then, I couldn't even imagine going on a plane to somewhere like London or Tel Aviv or Grand Rapids, Michigan. Simply exploring an open field with my sisters or looking for shells on a beach was thrilling. Every step enlarged my world.

The smog was so bad in Los Angeles when I was a kid, I couldn't see the mountains or the skyscrapers downtown. Sometimes the thick air obscured even the flag at the fire station down the street. At night the light pollution was so bright, I never knew what stars looked like. Heck, the flood lights at the park next to my apartment building stayed on until ten o'clock so the guys could play soccer after work, and I was asleep long before that.

The first time I saw stars on a camping trip, I couldn't breathe.

At the time, my world was so small: school, church, the block where I lived. When the skies opened to reveal *all that*, the immensity overwhelmed me.

I had been aware of the presence of God at a very young age. I had felt his presence with me when I was afraid or lonely or curious, but his presence had always been personal, intimate.

At night, camping near the redwoods of Sequoia National Park, I left our tent, flashlight in hand, to find a place to pee. Stepping out of our tent, I saw some of God's best work: stars. When I looked at the stars, I realized how grand he is. The infinity of it all overwhelmed me. That first time I could see stars, I could also see the Milky Way. I recognized it immediately from books and *National Geographic* magazines. I didn't know you could actually see it.

Far from the Los Angeles skyline, I was mesmerized by the resplendent universe stretched beyond me revealing just how small I was in this vast, immeasurable space. It was terrifying but thrilling. God unfolded, pressed, pulled, and formed this infinite world yet still remembered me. I exist not only as a thought but a body that moves and breathes and aches. God held that hazy spill of stars in the palm of his hand but cared for me too. In the moment it took one of those stars to wink at me, I knew I was loved, that I existed to be loved by the Creator. I felt the Spirit move over me like fingers caressing my hair. And then it vanished.

When I left my own neighborhood, it wasn't only in nature that God revealed himself to me, but also in meeting new people.

Once, when I was about nine, a school bus pulled up at the campsite next to ours. This bus wasn't yellow like the one I took to school but covered with flowers and butterflies in a myriad of colors. I couldn't see in the windows, as some of them had curtains. When the driver came to a stop, six children, from ages four to fourteen, jumped out. They eyed me and my sisters, perhaps to see if we were worth talking to and if any of us were their age. A few of the older boys started kicking rocks and jumping up on logs, when I noticed a little girl with uneven dirty blonde hair approaching us. Her two front teeth were missing, so I figured she was closer to my younger sister's age than mine, but it was me she wanted to talk to.

She didn't so much talk as ask rapid-fire questions. I had

a million for her too, like did she live in that bus? And how many sisters and brothers did she have? I noticed her mom climb out of the bus with a baby on her hip. But I didn't ask my questions because she wanted to know about me. Were there any more kids than just us? How old were we? Where were we from? Was my hair really red? Did I like strawberry milkshakes? Had I ever been to Disneyland?

Soon we found out we both collected stickers, and before I knew it, she was asking my mom if I could come to her bus to see her sticker collection—something I never would have asked.

She did live in that school bus. There were places to sleep and sit and even a stove inside. It was cramped and dark and a little bit dirty. We leafed through each other's sticker collections, stickers stuck or taped to the pages. We scratched and sniffed the ones that smelled and rubbed our fingers against the ones with sparkles. I thought of how incredibly different we lived but also how much we had in common. Then, like a gust of wind went through the bus, I saw that God loved her so very much. Just like I knew he loved me. I could tell she loved her family fiercely but was open to new things. God relished in her little questions and thought her hair, which looked like it had been cut with kitchen scissors, was adorable. I knew this because he helped me see it too.

Now, I know this is true and maybe even a bit obvious. But when you are in your own room, house, neighborhood, community, you forget that other people exist—people who are different from you. Sometimes you see them on television, where they become a character or, more so, a caricature of a person. You forget how *real* they are. And how much God delights in them too.

Travel always reminds me of this. Moments like this will happen in a flash, but I can recall them easily.

A young man with Down syndrome in the back of a shuttle bus waved to me in a piazza in Lucca, Italy.

A man wearing an Ohio State sweatshirt in Westminster Abbey was so overwhelmed by its grandeur, he was on the verge of tears and confided in me, a stranger, that he was frightened he'd forget it all like his mother with Alzheimer's forgot everything.

An elderly couple in Modena, Italy, blatantly watched my husband and me as we drank espresso and read. She in sensible black shoes and a bright blue skirt and jacket with matching blue purse set in the center of the table, a scarf tied around its handle. He with a cane and in pants pulled up to his armpits, letting his sockless ankles breathe. They stared at us, and they didn't even try to hide it—and I love them for it.

I find myself thinking this often as I people-watch during travel: "I love them," but better yet, "God loves them."

Without a word or a nod to mark the time to go, the couple rose at the same instant to leave. They said goodbye to the shopkeep and that they would see him tomorrow. As they walked down the alley, the bell chimed from the church nearby. I had the feeling they did this every afternoon and that the church bell set its time to them, not the other way around.

It is good to know there are more people in the world than just me, with ways of moving and living and existing in this world other than the way I do.

I didn't know what I was in for that first plane ride when I was twenty-five. I had moved from Los Angeles to Portland the previous year, towing my car on the back of a seventeen-foot-long U-Haul that was much too large for my meager belongings (mostly books) and driving to the Great Northwest. The following Thanksgiving I found a frighteningly low-cost plane ticket on a new website called Priceline. I told everyone—from the ticket agent to the flight attendant—it was my first flight, perhaps because I was a little afraid but mostly because I was excited.

When the plane took off, the sensation was much like the Knott's roller coasters I rode as a kid. In this vast new landscape of flight, I clenched the armrests for support, but the woman seated next to me reached out her hand for me to hold. Her hand was cool and firm. Holding it, I wasn't afraid anymore. The imprint of God within her reached out to care for me.

I knew then I was going to love to travel.

32

in abundance

1. The shivering moan of a cello
2. The way Katharine Hepburn was Katharine Hepburn
3. Warm towels straight out of the dryer
4. The messy mop of hair on a highland cow
5. Dahlias: the order of the entire universe in one single flower
6. Picking hot, sweet blackberries right off the vine
7. When a baby you do not know smiles at you
8. The clean, new beginning of a fresh haircut
9. Lotion between your toes
10. Everything to do with the season of fall
11. The first sip of morning coffee
12. The deep growl of the trumpet in Duke Ellington's music
13. When your child calls you "Mommy"
14. Continental accents
15. The hope of sunrise
16. The majesty and glory of bald eagles

17. The feeling in your soul when you sing with a crowd
18. The way the scent of peppermint cleanses everything
19. Kissing in the rain
20. Walking in the rain
21. Falling asleep to the sound of rain
22. Pretty much anything that has to do with rain
23. The dreamy sound of young Frank Sinatra singing with the Tommy Dorsey Orchestra
24. The glory of a new friendship in adulthood
25. The stillness of an Edward Hopper painting
26. The ruckus pop of a champagne cork
27. The honor of witnessing a butterfly dance in your yard
28. The haunting smell of a wood fire blazing in one of your neighbor's fireplaces
29. The sight of your loved one picking you up at the airport, even though you knew they were coming, expected them to come, but the sight of them is still devastatingly wonderful
30. The musical runs of Sam Cooke
31. The way your body, mind, and spirit feel after a hard laugh
32. The versatility of chicken salad
33. The fact that Cary Grant existed
34. The dizzying effect of a Vincent van Gogh painting
35. Sequoias' magnificent majesty
36. Tomatoes that taste like the sun itself
37. When Louis Armstrong hits a high note on his trumpet
38. Making a clear, straight cut on a roll of wrapping paper

39. The thrill of seeing a rainbow
40. The musty scent of an old book
41. The friend that makes jams and gives you jars of it
42. Sleeping with the heater on but the window open
43. The sound of a sharp pencil on paper
44. When a child who does not belong to you takes you by the hand
45. That the Welsh flag has a dragon on it
46. The way some people missed their artistic calling but it manifests itself in their charcuterie trays
47. The contagious laughter of a baby
48. The *pop* that occurs when you break a vacuum seal
49. The canine commotion of a dog park
50. Your teeth, not *before* or *during* a teeth cleaning but *afterward*. Who knew teeth could be so smooth?
51. How black-faced sheep look like stuffed animals
52. How sometimes you can't hear church because so many babies are cooing and jabbering and you remember Jesus said, "Let all the children come unto me," and you know you and those kids are right where you ought to be
53. The annual surprise and shock of the colors of autumn
54. Pandas, the lovable doofuses of nature
55. The feeling of a smooth, flat rock in your hand
56. People who know how to whistle with their fingers like a New Yorker
57. The sleepy shuffle of feet when you first wake
58. The way staring at a campfire seems to cleanse your mind
59. The sound of frogs croaking outside your window

60. The stir you feel when you identify a star correctly
61. A short, swift run to awaken your body, mind, and spirit
62. That there are men and women who have given their entire lives to pray for us
63. The wit and wisdom of Jane Austen
64. How we used to make mixtapes to share who we were with someone
65. The two-and-a-half-octave surprise opening of Gershwin's "Rhapsody in Blue"
66. The shoebill stork: a visitor from prehistoric times
67. The silence of staring at the ocean
68. The smell of a brand-new human baby
69. Finding a photo you've never seen before of a loved one who has died
70. The view from the top of a mile-high hike on a crisp autumn day
71. Skipping rocks across water
72. The gracious fading light of sunset
73. Finding the first bloom of spring after a particularly long, cold, dark winter
74. The sight of a horse, baby or adult, who had horrid accident walk for the first time
75. The warmth of seeing a home lit up with light from the inside
76. Seeing the flag of your country waving in the wind after you've been away for a long time
77. Having a glass of something delicious at sunset with friends on a porch
78. Lines in freshly cut grass

79. Lines in freshly vacuumed carpet
80. Rubbing your fingers on a rosemary bush when out on a walk
81. The anticipation of a tulip
82. Cracking a sheet of ice that has formed on the earth
83. Extinguishing a long match into a pile of sand
84. Sleeping under the love of a homemade quilt
85. The promise of a songbird chorus
86. Air conditioning in a Palm Springs summer
87. The way light looks coming through slatted blinds
88. Pulling out an old Christmas ornament that has been in your family for years
89. The crisp crunch of leaves under your feet
90. Tapping the ash off a cigar
91. Eating yogurt or ice cream with the perfect spoon
92. The time warp of tree rings
93. The smell of laundry dried out of doors
94. The magic of full moons
95. A perfect, clean pull of the first tissue, without tearing or breaking, right out of the box
96. The terrific thrill of a thunderstorm
97. The pride of finishing a thousand-piece puzzle
98. Placing the last piece into a jigsaw puzzle
99. Starting a new journal
100. The long shadow in the late afternoon of a sunny day

Abundance is all around us. The items in this list do not cost anything. They are not for the rich and famous. They simply are. They exist out there in the world. One just needs to look.

Abundance is simply a way of perceiving.

I started this list as I began to write this book. It occurred to me that when I looked for joy, I saw it everywhere.

My family knew I was creating this list, and many times as we shared a moment that might have gone under the radar, one of my sons would say, "You've got to put this one on 'the list'!"

Abundance begets abundance. I hope that your cup, too, will runneth over.

33

birthday joy

I love my birthday.

I love it a little more than the average person does.

Because my birthday is a week before Christmas, if I don't get excited about it, no one will.

Yes, I've had a *Sixteen Candles* birthday. You know, the 1980s Molly Ringwald film where no one remembers her sixteenth birthday? That has happened to me a few times.

On my worst birthday, my eighteenth, there was a bill under my bedroom door when I woke up, letting me know how much I owed in rent and utilities now that I was an adult.

I was still in high school.

Now I make certain no one forgets my birthday and that it is a blast for all who want to participate.

If you follow me on social media, you already know this. I post reminders with both goofy and cute pictures of me throughout the years. I begin these reminders one month before my birthday, then three weeks, then two, with a final countdown crescendo the last week.

Over the top? *Yes.*

Annoying? *Yes.*

It has become a day when I give others free rein to make fun of me, and many do, for my preferred gift is a shared memory from our life together. My childhood best friend shares a precious photo of the two of us in kindergarten. She dressed as a Pilgrim, and I as a Native American with two other girls, recalled to our memory in vivid tenderness on my birthday. A classmate from high school Civ Ed class says every time she hears the band a-ha's "Take On Me," she thinks of me. And a man I waited tables with during college reminds me of an elderly customer who would give me a dollar just for escorting him to his table. No refusal was allowed. Yes, he needed help getting to the table, but he wanted to pay you for it!

On my birthday I hear from my elementary school teachers, old bosses, the guy I had a crush on when I was fourteen, a seminary buddy who now lives in South Korea, and a family member who checks in only once a year—on my birthday.

Sometimes friends make memes at my expense, like one with a picture of three-year-old me, snatched off Facebook with "Birthday Is Coming Motto of House of Gonzalez" superimposed over the picture. Or a meme of my sixth-grade yearbook picture—teased bangs, braces, and all—warning all to "Be mature. It's my birthday!"

We all laugh at the ridiculousness of my birthday but also the joy—the joy of a life lived—together.

I've had many criticisms through the years. Some people do not understand what I try to do with my birthday. They find it self-indulgent or narcissistic. This is to miss the point, which is how much each person makes a difference in the lives of those around them. My birthday isn't about me making a difference in their life but them making a difference in mine.

Because of the countdown, I often receive a stack of cards in the mail, which I open slowly, cherishing each note and sometimes a treat sent. It takes two to three hours to open them all, for I send a text or social media message to each giver to let them know I received the card and what I loved most about it.

Yes, I do receive presents. Friends and family know I am even thrilled about a tube of lip balm in wrapping paper, so they send cookies and books and all my favorite things, but it is the connection that is the real gift. I receive phone calls with birthday wishes or a five-minute hello on their way to errands. Some make dates for lunch, coffee, walk, or dinner. When it is all over, I send out handwritten notes to all who participated in some way. Each gesture in this celebration, no matter how small, connects us once more, for another year.

The birthday celebration serves too as a part of my *memento mori* meditation. Borrowed by early Christians from the Greek Stoics, *memento mori* is translated from Latin as "remember you will die." *Memento mori* brings the refrain from Ash Wednesday, "Remember you are dust, and to dust you will return," to our everyday life. These words served as spiritual instruction through medieval times to the Victorian era—for those who fought in battle, those who went to sea, women in childbirth, and those experiencing the trials of everyday life.

We remember we will die, so that we will live—well.

In the last century, we've become removed from death. Death now often happens out of sight. To speak of death is taboo—so much so that grieving has become a private burden we carry alone.

But for us Christians, if we really believe what we say we believe, why would we be frightened?

The spiritual practice of *memento mori* confronts death until we no longer find it frightening. Some practice this discipline in prayer or by placing a skull in a place of prominence as a reminder. For my family, we visit cemeteries on our vacations. Our walks among graves remind us that one day we will die, and in doing so, we embrace life.

The spiritual practice of *memento mori* forces us to face mortality every day. In facing it, we begin to live more intentionally. We think about where we spend our time, our resources, our energy. Doing good work at our job or in the home takes on a new importance, as does sharing our love with those around us. I look at each day as if it might be my last, for truly, we never know. All we are given is today. So live it as well as you can, filled with life and love and joy. *Memento mori* challenges us to look at each day before us as a gift—one we don't want to waste.

Birthdays bring this practice into clearer focus: It might be my last birthday. A birthday is a good occasion to be intentional about such things, to amplify the goodness and community in my life. Don't wait until I am dead to tell me you love or appreciate me. And I won't wait to tell you either. It is a day to refocus on how truly abundant a life we live.

Because of this intentional practice, on my birthday every

single small act of kindness, from my husband making my morning coffee in a tumbler to go, to the first song that comes on the radio being one of my favorites of all time, to scoring my favorite parking spot, seems like a gift—because it is. Through the lens of my birthday, I am able to see that they are gifts, daily grace in the grace of my life.

I remember a video that went viral a few Christmases ago. In the video a man wakes up in the morning to find himself wrapped as a present. He pulls the paper off his face and shouts with joy "I'm alive!" He looks over to the other side of the bed to see his wife also wrapped as a present. "You're here too! I love you!" It goes on as his children are wrapped too. Light switches, water spigots, his shoes, breakfast—all are wrapped. We laugh at the silliness of it all until we finally begin to see, yes, all of this is a gift. This life is a gift.

Since my birthday is a week before Christmas, it often coincides with the third Sunday of Advent, Gaudete Sunday, the Sunday of Rejoicing. Gaudete Sunday reminds us that Christ is near: not just that it is almost the celebration of Christmas but also that he is returning soon to redeem us all and that he is here right now in our midst, Emmanuel, God with us.

Each of the readings of Gaudete Sunday is joyful. We sing, "Rejoice! Again I say: Rejoice!" during the processional. It is Saint Paul's call to the church of Philippi, even as he wrote under house arrest awaiting a death sentence, as if to say, "I am not dead yet! So I rejoice!" And instead of a responsorial psalm on Gaudete Sunday, we sing Mary's response to the angel Gabriel at the annunciation: "Magnificat! My soul rejoices in the Lord!" Mary rejoiced in the coming of the Messiah and that she got to play a part in it.

It is especially a gift when my birthday lies on Gaudete Sunday, for it reminds me I am not my own. I belong to the Lord. My life is a gift from him. Somehow I get to play a small part in his story of redemption and love. It reminds me of the refrain from Walt Whitman's "O Me! O Life!"

> That you are here—that life exists and identity,
> That the powerful play goes on, and you may
> contribute a verse.[1]

In church I sing the responses with full voice and gratitude for my full, rich, real, awkward, painful, tragic, hysterical, and beautiful life.

Life is a gift.

34

in sunsets

It was one of those days when I was feeling sorry for myself. Then I felt horrible for feeling sorry for myself because I was on a month-long solo trip to England to meditate on joy. But well, I wasn't feeling very joyful.

The past month had been one of the best months of my entire life. I'd experienced joy and God's presence in a way I never had before. I felt God close as I wandered the countryside, as I talked to strangers and looked at churches and farmland, old stone houses and sheep. But on this particular day, just a few before I was scheduled to return home, I was feeling sorry for myself. Not because the trip was coming to an end but because I missed my family—fiercely.

I wondered what they were doing at that very moment. With the eight-hour difference, they were probably all asleep. But I would have been happy to watch them sleep! Even though my youngest son is twelve, he still sleeps with a menagerie of stuffed animals. Sometimes it is difficult to find him in the pile of tigers, cows, capybaras, and even regular old teddy bears. "He's probably sleeping on his stomach, his pillow full of drool," I thought. How did *drool* make me homesick?

Then I thought, "My teenage son has probably fallen asleep with his portable speaker playing a podcast softly." He's at the age where he likes to listen to men talk about manly stuff, like lifting weights and drinking protein shakes. I'm not sure if he will do any of those things any time soon, but he likes to keep his options open.

And my husband, my sweet husband, who made all of this possible, was sleeping alone in our bed. He was probably stretched out like a starfish, able to use all four corners of the bed without me taking up space and blankets. I'm sure he missed me, but he was probably getting the best sleep of his life.

The last week of the trip, I was in Bath, England. Bath is an ancient city with Roman foundations, just a little over an hour's train ride from London. Just as the Romans had finished building a magnificent spa here on the hot springs off the Avon River in AD 70, five thousand miles away the temple in Jerusalem was again destroyed. Both places paid tribute to the same emperor during a time when the first stirrings of Christianity were planted within his hold. The ruins of the Roman bath are still in Bath, but the city is most known for its Georgian townhomes. Jane Austen lived in Bath for five years. She hated it, but *Persuasion* and *Northanger Abbey* are both partly set in the city. When I see the Georgian architecture, I can't help but think of Austen and the characters she brought to life.

During this trip it was my practice to attend a church

service in the morning, write, and then take a long walk after lunch. On this day, the one when I felt sorry for myself, I decided to be a glutton for punishment. My long walk would be to an abandoned cemetery I noticed on the map. I know it sounds morbid, but I enjoy going to cemeteries. They remind me that my life is but a breath. While I am here, I am to live well and love well. A cemetery would be just the thing to cheer me up.

I hiked out of the city and through the surrounding canals, forest, and farmland to arrive at the abandoned Smallcombe Cemetery. These grounds have not been open to new burials since the late 1980s; most of the graves are from the late nineteenth century. The early February wind was bitter in the shade of the trees. Many of the graves still had early-morning frost covering them in the middle of the day. Those laid to rest surrounded a dilapidated masonry church whose roof caved in long ago. Among the graves were the parents of poet A. E. Housman and their seven children, sans A. E., two Victoria Cross recipients, soldiers from WWI and the Zulu wars, and a headstone with the name of Frederick Weatherly, composer of "Danny Boy," upon it.

I hummed the pipey tune to myself as I walked among the dead. Despite the sun in the clearing, among the graves there was an icy chill in the air. I could see my breath and often had to rub my fingers to get the circulation going. As much as I love imagining the lives of those who have lived before me, the cemetery hadn't cheered me up. I decided it was time to head back.

Instead of a straight out and back, I decided to make a loop and cover different ground. I'd heard there was a lookout at the top of the crest, Bath Skyline, where one could see the entire city stretched out before them.

I headed back, still thinking about my family, who were probably just waking for the day. I could nearly hear our one-hundred-year-old steps creaking under their weight as they each headed down the stairs to brush teeth or to start the coffee.

As I approached the lookout, I slipped in my earbuds and scrolled Spotify to find Mahler's Ninth Symphony, his last symphony, the perfect soundtrack to my moodiness. Some say Mahler wrote the symphony as he grieved the death of his daughter Maria Anna. Some say he wrote it after a heart disease diagnosis. He would never hear it performed. He died shortly after its completion.

But I didn't hear all that.

I reached the crest of the hill, and the skyline spanned an area the length of two football fields. Only a handful of people distanced across the field. I lifted my eyes to the city before me. I could see the steeple of Bath Abbey, the five-hundred-year-old Gothic church where I had been attending evening prayers. In fact, just two days before, when no priest showed up to lead prayers, I had been allowed to do so. The honor had overwhelmed me. I, a woman who grew up in East Los Angeles on government cheese, got to lead prayers at Bath Abbey. I saw the train station where I had arrived a week before after weeks in the remote, quiet countryside with Benedictine monks. And I saw hundreds, if not thousands, of Georgian buildings in the same uniform height and sandstone color in miles of expanse.

And then, as if choreographed to the strings soaring

in my ears, the light in the sky began to darken. Streaks of periwinkle blue, then purple, splashed across the breadth of the sky. Clouds spun pink and sherbet as if they were made of cotton candy. All I was witnessing moved in sync with the music, the notes made manifest as brushstrokes in the sky. And then I knew, this symphony wasn't about dying; it was about living.

Writer and theologian Frederick Buechner told a story about showing up to teach a class one evening when he noticed a sensational sunset beginning outside. Without saying a word, he switched off the classroom light and faced the west windows. The lively conversation among the students faded as, one by one, each student turned toward the fading light. For twenty minutes silence sat over the room as "we watched one day of our lives come to an end."[1]

On the top of that hill, tears streamed down my cheeks. This time not from sadness or loneliness but because I could see it now: my thorny childhood and the sensitivity it cultivated, my love of literature and music, my cozy home back in Seattle, which holds our unexpected but lasting love, and—on this final day of my journey—the revelation that my core desire is to know the God who has cradled me through it all. God had been painting a picture I didn't even know was there.

And then I couldn't stop smiling and crying and nodding my head yes and laughing. It was as if God wanted me to witness this sunset to get my attention, to really, truly see that all the moments of the trip—monks, strangers, liturgy, train rides, leading prayers, sheep, and walking among graves—had been leading me to this moment, a painting of my life.

35

in the face of death

First-century Rome. A man sits in a dark room alone, furiously scribbling a letter. He has not left his home in days, weeks, months even. He can't leave, for there is an armed centurion at his door. The man is a follower of Jesus awaiting certain execution for his faith by the monstrous Roman emperor, Nero. He knows his time on this earth is ending. He sends out a correspondence to some of the people he loves and writes down these words:

"Rejoice in the Lord always. I will say it again: Rejoice!"[1]

This does not sound like a man in the throes of desperation. He does not sound frightened or scared—because he's not. This is a man who has spent years attuning his lens to the presence of God's grace in his life. This man is Saint Paul.

When I struggle with my faith and begin to wonder if there is any truth to it at all, when I call out, "Lord, help my unbelief!," I find myself in the book of Philippians, a letter gushing with happiness, love, and hope. And when I think about the story behind it all, the letter becomes one of revelation. Paul's joyful certainty in the face of death is more than inspiring; it is real faith.

Saint Paul's story—how he got to the place where he is joyfully awaiting death—is enough to make me believe. In today's terms, Paul had been the equivalent of an ISIS fighter. He despised Christians; he was known for persecuting them. Paul was present at the stoning of the first martyr, Stephen, and it's the first time we read of Paul in Scripture. Paul stood there as the mob hurled stones at Stephen, crushing his bones and his skull, until his lifeless body was obscured by them. And Paul stood there approving "of their killing him."[2]

Hunting down Christians became Paul's life work, how he found value in himself. Being anti-Christian was Paul's identity. Scripture says while Paul "was still breathing out murderous threats against the Lord's disciples" and writing letters to other Pharisees asking if they had found any Christians so he "might take them as prisoners,"[3] he had an experience with the risen Lord.

On the road to Damascus, blinded by a flash of light from heaven, Paul heard the voice of Jesus ask him, "Why do you persecute me?" I love this, for it foreshadows the theology Paul teaches later—that we Christians are connected by body and spirit to Jesus. Jesus didn't ask why Paul was persecuting those who believe in him, but Jesus himself. We are his body.

Dumbfounded, Paul asked, "Who are you?"

Jesus repeated that it was he: "Jesus, whom you are persecuting."

Jesus told Paul to go into the city and wait. Blinded from that flash from heaven, Paul couldn't see. The encounter was short. Jesus said only a few words to Paul and then, in his kindness, gave Paul time to sit with those words. He did not eat or drink. He sat in the dark—and waited—for three days.

I don't know why, but this part of the story makes me laugh. I wonder what was going through Paul's mind during those three days. His entire identity as the man who hunts down Christians because what they believe is untrue is demolished. It is true! The risen Lord has revealed himself to Paul, the man who hated Christians! Paul's entire identity was shaken.

And then Jesus sent a guide, a believer whose name, Ananias, means, "the Lord shows grace." Ananias didn't want to see Paul, let alone comfort and encourage him. He'd heard Paul was a terror and knew of the horrors he had inflicted on Christians. But Jesus told Ananias, "This man is my chosen instrument. . . . I will show him how much he must suffer for my name."[4]

Knowing how much Paul did indeed suffer for Christ, I want to know what he experienced in that flash of light, in those few words. What gave him so much hope and security and assurance that he would someday once again be with Christ?

I think of Mother Teresa, now Saint Teresa of Calcutta, whose journals were released posthumously. These journals revealed that she did not feel God's presence throughout her life. All her sacrifice and work and devotion were based on one experience she had in her youth when she heard Christ's voice clearly. Her life was one of struggle and suffering, but that one experience was enough to compel her, knowing that one day she would experience his presence again.

Paul was willing—not begrudgingly but powerfully,

joyously willing—to go through everything from a beating, to a stoning, an imprisonment, a shipwreck, and now an impending execution because he not just hoped but was confident—no, *knew*—he would be with Christ once again.

And this is where we find our hero, our saint, at the beginning of Philippians.

In the previous year, Paul had been put on trial in Caesarea for his preaching. Knowing the Pharisees planned on ambushing and murdering him if he was taken to Jerusalem, Paul appealed to Festus that as a Roman citizen, he should be sent to Rome instead.

The journey to Rome was a cinematic adventure suited for Hollywood. There was a terrific storm so terrible the sailors no longer fought it. They simply gave way, and the ship was tossed about. When the storm subsided, the sailors passed ropes under the vessel to keep the boat from falling apart.

Paul told everyone on board not to be afraid, for an angel appeared to him and let him know not one person would be lost from the ship. He had a tremendous amount of calm as seasoned sailors scrambled around him.

After two weeks of storms and chaos, some of the sailors tried to abandon ship on the lifeboats. Paul talked a centurion into cutting the ties to the lifeboats, saying that unless everyone stayed together, they would not be saved. The next morning, they saw land. There was no port, so the sailors put up the sail and made a break for the beach. The vessel progressed closer to shore but was broken to pieces. They got to land by holding on to "planks or on other pieces of the ship."[5]

It was like one of those action movies where everything

keeps going wrong. When they reached the shore, it was pouring. The men attempted to build a fire in the downpour. When they finally got the fire roaring, a poisonous viper was driven out of the kindling by the heat. The snake fastened itself to Paul's hand. But Paul's arm did not swell. He did not die, so the men decided Paul must be a god.

They had landed on the island of Malta, and they had to wait three months for another ship. Paul, still a prisoner, was finally transported to Rome and put under house arrest, where he would stay for two years. It is here that he pens a thank-you letter to the church at Philippi for a gift they sent him.

I understand that Paul didn't want to be killed by the Pharisees and that is why he appealed to Rome. But why did he appeal to Rome knowing it was Emperor Nero he would appeal to? Some say it is because Nero had not yet begun his terror on Christians, so Paul didn't know how sadistic Nero could or would be. But I think it was for the very reason he shares in this letter to the Philippians: "What has happened to me has actually served to advance the gospel."[6] He trusted Jesus so much that he knew God would carry him through the trials he experienced on land and sea and that his trials would bring others to know Jesus too. He wanted to visit Rome to "bear some fruit." He wanted to convert Rome. All these trials made this possible.

Paul writes that others have "become confident in the Lord and dare all the more to proclaim the gospel without fear"[7] Some did so because they were jealous of Paul. But in all of this, Paul rejoices. Paul expects that he will not be put to shame and that whether he lives or dies, "Christ will be exalted."[8] Paul reminds the church not to be "frightened in any way by those who oppose you."[9]

Paul's letter drips with happiness, positivity, and enthusiasm. Paul uses a version of the word *joy* sixteen times in these four short chapters. "Always pray with joy,"[10] he writes, and "Because of this I rejoice!" and "I will continue to rejoice"[11] and "Rejoice with me!" and "Welcome him in the Lord[12] with great joy." His joy is infectious. It is a result of his intimacy with God. Joy isn't about circumstances; it is the lens through which he views the world.

Paul could have been bitter. Jaded even. But in a situation where it seems that all his independence and autonomy have been taken from him, the words he pens breathe freedom: "If you have any encouragement from being united with Christ," be united.[13] He reminds his friends to let their joy and love overflow, to imitate Christ's humility:

> Who, being in very nature God,
> did not consider equality with God something
> to be used to his own advantage;
> rather, he made himself nothing
> by taking the very nature of a servant,
> being made in human likeness.
> And being found in appearance as a man,
> he humbled himself
> by becoming obedient to death—
> even death on a cross![14]

These verses might very well be my favorite in all of Scripture. They are rich in theology, poetic in nature, and a practical reminder for me when my head simply gets too big. I am reminded of the words to a Keith Green song my parents played when I was a child

> My reward is not a crown but giving glory to you.

Paul writes to the church in Philippi that if they live out their faith "without grumbling or arguing,"[15] overflowing with love, they will shine like stars in the universe. They will give glory to God. And for that, Paul rejoices.

I think Paul knew he was nearing the end. He looks over his life, reminding the Philippians what he came from: "circumcised on the eighth day, of the people of Israel, of the tribe of Benjamin, a Hebrew of Hebrews; in regard to the law, a Pharisee."[16] He had the right pedigree. He came from the right people. He was educated in the right schools. And he reminds them that it was he who persecuted the church. But all of this is nothing compared to knowing Christ and to "be found in him."[17]

It is as if Paul is saying, "Come on, you guys! You know who I was, who I've been." But Christ is Paul's identity now. Not the right breeding or education. Not his activism.

I relate to this. Sometimes I am so grateful for the goodness of God's grace in my life, I want to remind my friends and family and myself, "You guys, remember how I used to be afraid all the time? Remember how I didn't want to leave the house, and any source of conflict would make me take to my bed?" But knowing Christ has changed all that. Now Christ is my identity. Not my anxiety or the abuse in my past.

Our true identity is in being connected to Christ—knowing him and the power of his resurrection and sharing in his suffering. Paul pleas with the church to join him in this calling. Because of our connection to Christ, we can rejoice.

Rejoice in the Lord always. I will say it again: Rejoice!

It is because of Christ that we can be happy in suffering, joyful in trials, filled with "peace of God which transcends all understanding."[18]

"To live is Christ and to die is gain," Paul writes confidently.[19]

Two hundred fifty years after Nero executed Paul, the roman emperor Constantine converted to Christianity and legalized the religion in Rome. Paul wouldn't know how much his suffering and preaching of the gospel grew the church in Rome. He was basking in the glowing love of his Savior.

36

don't be such a Pollyanna!

"Don't be such a Pollyanna!"

People say this all the time, often to anyone who shows a semblance of cheerfulness, positivity, or joy. Yes, sometimes people say this to me.

People say "Pollyanna" as if the name is synonymous with someone flighty. Someone who does not know the ways of the world. Someone who is blissfully, ignorantly cheerful. This is the furthest thing from the truth.

Maybe you saw the Disney movie on cable when you were young. Or perhaps you read the book, originally published in 1913 by Eleanor H. Porter, which, as always, is better than the movie.

Let me refresh your memory.

Pollyanna is a missionary girl who has lost both her mother and father by the time she is eleven years old. She's pawned off to her closest living relative: an unkind, unwelcoming, self-righteous, wealthy aunt. The aunt makes it clear she doesn't want Pollyanna, but it is her duty to take her in. Despite living alone in the largest, fanciest house in the town, the aunt places Pollyanna in the smallest, most inhospitable room, next to the attic. Pollyanna doesn't point out what the room lacks—it has a bare floor and walls—but immediately points out what is pleasant in the room: a small window. She can look out to the trees and houses of the town and can even see the church spire.

When I was a child, my parents fought often. Nearly each year, my mother would have enough and leave my father, then later take him back. So nearly every year, my mother, my two sisters, and I moved to a new rented house. Each one was worse than the last, small and stuffy and riddled with cockroaches. Each time we moved, my sisters and I set out to find the one pleasant thing about the new place. One had a "Mister Rogers" window by the front door. We called it that, for just like Mister Rogers, we could look through it to see who was knocking. Another did not have grass in the backyard but a concrete pad. We discovered this was a great place to ride our bikes in circles.

When Pollyanna chooses not to focus on the storage trunks piled outside her door that remind her she is in the far reaches of the house, where things are stored and forgotten, I understand. It doesn't help. Anyone can look at what is bad. It takes a special little girl to focus on what is good.

Pollyanna's father died two weeks prior to her moving to her aunt's house. The girl is grieving, alone, and unwelcome. When she first mentions her father, her aunt tells her she is not to mention him anymore. Eyes brimming with tears,

Pollyanna internalizes this demand, as perhaps her aunt knows best and in her "kindness" has told her not to speak of her father. Perhaps it'll be easier if she doesn't talk about him.

Of course, it is still difficult. On that first evening at her aunt's, Pollyanna consoles herself by exploring the field behind the house. She finds comfort in this wide-open space, sitting on a grand rock, watching the sky turn shades of red as the sun sets. So distracted is she that she misses dinner. Her aunt orders all the food to be packed away.

The aunt is unaffected by her niece's absence, but the housemaid and solace to Pollyanna, Nancy, is concerned, goes to find her, and sneaks the girl a snack before bed. It is here that Pollyanna confides in Nancy about the "Glad Game."

The Glad Game is something she and her father played when things didn't go exactly as planned. Once, the missionary barrel—a barrel packed with odds and ends others thought it was their duty to send to help the missionaries—came with a pair of crutches instead of something they needed or wanted. Pollyanna's father reframed the disappointment: Be glad you don't need them.

It is this very tactic that Pollyanna returns to in her grief when she notices she is not welcome in her new home. She will be grateful. She will be joyful despite her aunt's constant reminders that anything she does is out of duty. Pollyanna will be defiantly joyful.

My sister has pointed this out in my own life. My sister says she doesn't worry about me. People may be cruel or unkind, but I never let it show that they have hurt me. I am joyful. When people reject me or thwart my plans, I only smile. It is an opportunity to grow, an opportunity to play the Glad Game. I point out those who are kind. I notice those who have encouraged me on my journey.

Pollyanna has this outlook as she integrates herself into the town community. The aunt has Pollyanna take over some of her duties, one of which is to bring food to Mrs. Snow, a shut-in who stays in bed all day in her dark room. Mrs. Snow is "cantankerous," and it is unclear if she is actually ill or just enjoys holding court from her bedroom, as she "had lived forty years, and for fifteen of those years she had been too busy wishing things were different to find much time to enjoy things as they were."[1] Everyone, including her grown daughter, tiptoes around the woman, but Pollyanna is too joyful for that.

Pollyanna is no stranger to broken people. Her father was a minister. His work was to tend to broken people, and his daughter worked alongside him. She learned to attune to actual suffering and the suffering people bring upon themselves.

Pollyanna heard that Mrs. Snow would complain about whatever food had been brought, regardless of whether she previously said it was her favorite. So when Mrs. Snow expresses her disappointment that Pollyanna has brought chicken instead of lamb, Pollyanna laughs right in her face. Not because she is "impertinent," as Mrs. Snow calls her, but because Pollyanna can see when one's outlook needs reframing.

I think this is why Pollyanna, and child characters like her, always appealed to me as a child. They were wise beyond their years and saw the right way to take hold of a situation. Any child who grows up in some sort of drama, or trauma, wants to feel like they have control of something. They sense that the adults in charge are just making a mess of it all. Even in elementary school, I noticed the pattern that my mother would take my abusive father back a few months after we settled into a new house. I wanted a new start for my mother and for us kids. Seeing my mother start the cycle all over again felt hopeless. When I read of Pollyanna or Anne of Green Gables taking control of a situation and changing an adult's heart for good, it gave me hope. When I was a grown up, I would know what was right and true.

During Pollyanna's first visit to Mrs. Snow, she opens the curtains, bringing light into the sick room, which prompts her to notice that Mrs. Snow is beautiful. She tells her as much. Pollyanna fluffs the pillows and sets out to fix Mrs. Snow's hair. By the time she leaves, Mrs. Snow is rejuvenated, feeling better in body and spirit, and Pollyanna has sown the seeds of her Glad Game. Mrs. Snow needed encouragement and a new perspective, not someone to coddle her sickness.

In this way, Pollyanna spreads her outlook to the entire town. She is not afraid of broken people: an orphan boy, the town curmudgeon. Even the town doctor admits the girl is the best medicine he could give his patients: "Her quaint speeches are constantly being repeated to me, and, as near as I can make out, 'just being glad' is the tenor of most of them."[2] He wishes he could "prescribe" Pollyanna.

It is clear that her aunt's sense of duty and decorum had spread a joyless film over the town. Nowhere has this sense of joyless doom been more prevalent than in church. The Reverend Paul Ford, "sick at heart," can only see the criticism, bickering, and suffering of his congregation and Christianity on the whole. He hasn't a clue how to encourage his congregation or himself. Rev. Ford focuses on the "woe unto you" texts of the Bible in his sermons, the fire-and-brimstone texts, until Pollyanna comes across him practicing his sermon among some trees outside of town.

Remembering that old look of frustration her own minister father sometimes held, she reminds Rev. Ford of the "rejoicing texts"—over eight hundred joyful texts in Scripture that call believers to "Be glad in the Lord" or "Rejoice greatly" or "Shout for joy."[3] Her father had told her, "If God took the trouble to tell us eight hundred times to be glad and rejoice, He must want us to do it." In this, Pollyanna transforms even the reverend as he commits to preaching on those eight hundred happy texts and is renewed in his vocation.

On the surface, it seems such a simple story of faith, but it is earth-shattering. Rev. Ford had forgotten the gospel. We forget the gospel. Despite sin and bickering, evil and death, orphans and war, child abuse and neglect, there is beauty and wonder and awe and hope. This is the gospel: We can live joyously through all of this, for our sorrows and suffering will be redeemed.

And of course, Pollyanna even wins over her aunt.

When tragedy strikes Pollyanna, the townspeople flood to her aunt's house to show their love and encouragement. Pollyanna's aunt hears of the marvels Pollyanna has accomplished, including turning down a more loving home because she didn't want to leave her aunt alone. Finally, her aunt recognizes how fearful the prospect of being without

Pollyanna could be. She asks Nancy to explain the Glad Game to her and realizes Pollyanna has brought peace and joy to the entire town.

Ten-year-old me felt vindicated reading this. Yes, we children do know how to fix things. Why doesn't anyone ask our opinion or thoughts? Why don't adults treat children like people?

My now teen sons have noticed this throughout their lives. They point out the singsongy way teachers and other adults have spoken to them. "It's like they think we are stupid, Mom. You've never talked to us like that. You always talked to us like we were people." I talked to them like this because I remember what it felt like, and I know children are capable of much more than we give them credit for.

The book ends with hope as an out-of-town doctor is able to heal Pollyanna, and her aunt finds love with the town doctor.

The light Pollyanna brings to this town is foreshadowed by a text the reverend reads from a magazine earlier in the story: "What men and women need is encouragement. . . . Instead of always harping on a man's faults, tell him of his virtues. . . . The influence of a beautiful, helpful, hopeful character is contagious and may revolutionize a whole town."[4]

This is exactly what Pollyanna did. Sometimes we just need someone to show us how. Pollyanna showed a town not to be afraid of themselves or each other. She guided an entire community out of victimhood and taught grown-ups that gratitude is necessary for living a joy-filled life. And in all of this, she taught herself resilience.

Not that I have lived a life even close to anything like Pollyanna's, but I do think the way I tried to reframe things when I was a child and the joy I practice fiercely now, as an adult, has built resilience.

I think of the old adage "Don't pray for patience, because you might not like the way you'll learn it."

I'd add "joy" to that adage. If you are going to meditate on joy, determined to write about joy as an act of defiance in the face of evil, you will be spiritually attacked.

During the year I wrote this book,

- My husband had an accident that rendered him unable to walk for months.
- I lost several writing positions within the church I had been involved with for years.
- My integrity and character were questioned by yet another long-term faith community.
- A man I had never met before decided to park the van he was living in right outside my house and then wait and watch for each time I left the house, even if it was four o'clock in the morning for the gym, to yell and holler and try to intimidate me.
- I experienced a loneliness I had not felt in years.
- Oh yeah, and all the electricity went out in our house, costing thousands to repair.

I am sure there are more and will be more, but these are the big ones I can remember.

I lost my footing with a few of these. It took me a while to realize what was going on. But at least in the case of the man parked in front of my house, I knew exactly what was going on. I said as much to the police officer who came to take my statement. I told him that I was a person of faith writing about joy as an act of defiance in the face of evil. Then I laughed because it all seemed so obvious and ridiculous. The police officer, shocked by my candor, revealed that he too was a person of faith. He had seen things that can only be attributed to the "things invisible" from the Nicene Creed. The two of us stood on my porch encouraged and connected for that moment.

And that loneliness, it drew me closer, is still drawing me closer, to Jesus in a new, powerful, and incredible way.

As I endured a few distresses—nothing burdensome, but troubles that would have derailed me before I decided to be resolute and keep my eyes on Christ—I began to understand why James wrote, "Consider it pure joy, my brothers and sisters, whenever you face trials of many kinds, because you know that the testing of your faith produces perseverance."[5] My perseverance did become more evident, and I did begin to feel that these "trials" were evidence of doing something right for Jesus.

And isn't this joy for reals? A joy you can clasp on the shoulders and hold it close, despite chaos circling? I'm not talking detachment or something flighty. I'm talking about focused, resolute, crystal-clear, you-can't-take-this-away-from-me *joy*. The kind of joy that knows who I belong to and that nothing can separate me from his love.

I have a long way to go, but I have learned so much. You might be tempted to call me a Pollyanna, but now that you know her true story and mine—that neither of us are blissfully ignorant of the difficulties of this world but that, like the excerpt from the reverend's magazine, we want to remind you of your virtues and inspire you to encourage, to influence, to be contagious, to revolutionize—you'll know I take the name proudly.

This itself seems like an act of rebellion.

acknowledgments

To Paul Pastor, for igniting a fire under my feet.

To my agent, Keely Boeving, for taking a chance.

To Rebecca Moon Ruark and Jeanne Kaplan, who dust my words and encourage my spirit.

To Jim Hainer, Mike and Kathy Freeman, and the monks of St. Martin's Abbey in Lacey, Washington, and St. Augustine's in Chilworth, England, who gave me refuge.

To Kyle Rohane, for understanding what I was attempting to do. And Kim Tanner, yes, there is joy in editing.

And to You. *Soli Deo gloria!* This is an act of worship I lay at Your altar. I will spend the rest of my life searching for this space with You again.

notes

Introduction

1. Nehemiah 8:10
2. Anne Sexton, "Welcome Morning," in *The Complete Poems of Anne Sexton* (Houghton Mifflin Co., 1999), 455.

Chapter 1: Of Naps

1. Wendell Berry, excerpt of ["The body in the invisible"] from *This Day: Collected and New Sabbath Poems 1979–2012.* Copyright © 1990 by Wendell Berry. Reprinted with the permission of The Permissions Company, LLC on behalf of Counterpoint Press, counterpointpress.com.
2. Berry, *This Day.*

Chapter 2: Joy as an Act of Defiance

1. Isaac Rosenberg, "Returning, We Hear the Larks," The Poetry Foundation, accessed June 22, 2024, https://www.poetry foundation.org/poems/57223/returning-we-hear-the-larks.
2. Matthew 14:22–36
3. Psalm 65:7–8
4. "Chefoo School," Wikipedia, Wikimedia Foundation, last modified August 8, 2024, 13:38 (UTC), https://en.wikipedia.org /wiki/Chefoo_School.
5. Based on Psalm 46:1
6. Mary Previte, "559: Captain's Log - This American Life," This American Life, December 14, 2017, https://www.thisamericanlife .org/559/transcript.

7. Previte, "559: Captain's Log - This American Life."
8. Philippians 1:12
9. Christian Wiman, ed., *Joy: 100 Poems* (Yale University Press, 2017), xxiii–xxix.

Chapter 3: In the Drive-Through Car Wash

1. This entire entry is a reprint of Shemaiah Gonzalez, "Prayer of Thanks for the Drive Thru Car Wash." *U.S. Catholic*, June 1, 2020, uscatholic.org/. Reprinted with permission by *U.S. Catholic. U.S. Catholic* is published by the Claretian Missionaries. Call 1-800 -328-6515 for subscription information.

Chapter 7: Of Wandering

1. Psalm 31:1
2. Psalm 130:6
3. Michel de Montaigne, *On Solitude* (Penguin Books, 2010), 14–15.

Chapter 8: In a Smile

1. Exodus 34:29–35
2. Romans 2:4
3. 2 Corinthians 2:15–16
4. 2 Corinthians 3:18

Chapter 9: In Van Gogh's *Sunflowers*

1. "10 Facts That You Don't Know About 'Sunflowers' by Van Gogh," VincentVanGogh.org, accessed October 18, 2024, https://www.vincentvangogh.org/sunflowers.jsp.
2. Emma Taggart, "5 Synesthesia Artists Who Paint Their Multi-Sensory Experiences," My Modern Met, March 1, 2019, https://mymodernmet.com/synesthesia-art/.
3. "297: To Theo Van Gogh. The Hague, Sunday, 31 December 1882 and Tuesday, 2 January 1883," Vincent Van Gogh Letters, accessed October 18, 2024, https://vangoghletters.org/vg/letters/let297/letter.html.
4. TED-Ed, "The Unexpected Math Behind Van Gogh's 'Starry Night' - Natalya St. Clair," October 30, 2014, YouTube, 4 min. 38 sec., https://www.youtube.com/watch?v=PMerSm2ToFY.

5. "Letter of August 2nd, 1890 The painter Emile Bernard describes the burial of Van Gogh to Albert Aurier, art critic," Bureau Heidi Vandamme, July 29, 2015, https://bureauheidivandamme.nl/wp-content/uploads/VanGogh-29July-2015-EN.pdf.

Chapter 10: In Laundry

1. Kathleen Norris, *The Quotidian Mysteries: Laundry, Liturgy, and "Women's Work"* (Paulist Press, 1998), 15.
2. Alice McDermott, *The Ninth Hour* (Farrar, Straus and Giroux, 2017), 41.
3. McDermott, *The Ninth Hour,* 41.
4. Norris, *The Quotidian Mysteries,* 15.
5. Norris, *The Quotidian Mysteries,* 22.
6. Norris, *The Quotidian Mysteries,* 22.
7. Deuteronomy 6:5
8. Deuteronomy 6:7
9. Norris, *The Quotidian Mysteries,* 16.
10. McDermott, *The Ninth Hour,* 154.

Chapter 11: Joyful Mary and Christ

1. Marina Gross-Hoy (@marinagrosshoy), "Tired moms in the Metropolitan Museum of Art in New York City," Instagram, September 20, 2022, https://www.instagram.com/reel/CiulmEvP96K/?utm_source=ig_web_copy_link&%3Bigshid=MzRlODBiNWFlZA%3D%3D.
2. Psalm 121:8
3. Matthew 6:26
4. Luke 1:38
5. Luke 1:44
6. Luke 1:47–48
7. Luke 2:19
8. This and the next four quotations are from Luke 2:46–52.

Chapter 12: Of the Sabbath

1. Exodus 20:8
2. Psalm 46:10
3. Based on Song of Solomon 2:4

Chapter 13: In Dreams of Loss

1. Bettie Jo Basinger, "Mahler Listening Guide | Symphony No. 2 in C Minor ('Resurrection')," Utah Symphony, November 6, 2014, https://utahsymphony.org/explore/2014/11/mahler-2-listening-guide/.

Chapter 15: Confessions of a Killjoy

1. Christian Wiman, "Faith Comes Through Hearing," *Commonweal Magazine*, November 15, 2020, https://www.commonwealmagazine.org/faith-comes-through-hearing.
2. John 10:10

Chapter 17: Of Compline

1. 2 Timothy 1:7 KJV
2. Melissa Musick and Anna Keating, *The Catholic Catalogue: A Field Guide to the Daily Acts That Make Up a Catholic Life* (Image, 2019), 69.
3. Musick and Keating, *The Catholic Catalogue*, 71.
4. Musick and Keating, *The Catholic Catalogue*, 71.
5. 1 Peter 5:8–9 RSV
6. © 1969, James Quinn SJ and Geoffrey Chapman, a Cassell imprint, Wellington House, Strand, London WC2R 0BB "Day is Done."
7. "Compline" © 1995, Society of the Sacred Mission, Willen Priory, Milton Keynes, Buckinghamshire.
8. Psalm 139:12

Chapter 18: Of Knowing You Are Small

1. Walt Whitman, "O Me! O Life!" in *Leaves of Grass* (Philadelphia, 1892), 229.
2. Acts 17:28
3. G. K. Chesterton, *Orthodoxy* (Canon Press, 2020), 16.

Chapter 19: Trumpet Joy

1. "Tributes," The Louis Armstrong Educational Foundation," accessed October 18, 2024, https://louisarmstrongfoundation.org/tributes/.

Chapter 24: In Food

1. Joy Harjo, "Perhaps the World Ends Here," in *The Woman Who Fell from the Sky* (W. W. Norton, 1994).
2. James H. Forest, *Praying with Icons* (Orbis Books, 2014), 99.
3. John 17:22–23
4. *Chef's Table*, season 6, episode 2, "Dario Cecchini," directed by Jimmy Goldblum, aired February 22, 2019, Netflix.
5. "BUTCHER SHOP," Dario Cecchini, accessed January 9, 2024, https://www.dariocecchini.com/butcher-shop-2/?lang=en.

Chapter 25: Of Musical Theater

1. Dr. Jordan B. Peterson, host, *The Dr. Jordan B. Peterson Podcast*, episode 241, "How Anti-Racism Is Hurting Black America | John McWhorter," April 4, 2022, 1:17:31, https://music.youtube.com/podcast/u9quq9NGUcM.

Chapter 26: Of the Urban Bestiary

1. Matthew 6:26–27
2. Lyanda Lynn Haupt, *The Urban Bestiary: Encountering the Everyday Wild* (Little, Brown, and Co., 2013), 4.
3. Haupt, *The Urban Bestiary*, 4.

Chapter 27: In the Darkest of Places

1. Corrie ten Boom with Elizabeth and John Sherrill, *The Hiding Place*, 35th anniversary edition (Chosen Books, 2006), 209.
2. 1 Thessalonians 5:16–18
3. 1 Thessalonians 5:17
4. Jeremiah 29:5–7
5. Romans 5:3–5

Chapter 28: In Silence

1. Blaise Pascal, *Pensées and Other Writings* (Oxford University Press, 2008), 44.
2. Psalm 46:10
3. Robert Cardinal Sarah with Nicholas Diat, *The Power of Silence: Against the Dictatorship of Noise* (Ignatius Press, 2017).

4. Psalm 62:1 AMP
5. Sarah, *Power of Silence*.
6. Francis Thompson, *The Works of Francis Thompson: Poems*, 2 vols. (Charles Scribner's Sons, 1913), 1:107–13.

Chapter 29: Of Coffee

1. Acts 17:27

Chapter 30: Of Books

1. L. M. Montgomery, *Anne of Green Gables* (Bantam Books, 1998), 33.
2. Ralph Waldo Emerson, *The Essential Writings of Ralph Waldo Emerson* (Modern Library, 2000), 134.
3. Henry David Thoreau, "Conclusion," in *Walden and Civil Disobedience*, Anthology of American Literature, (Simon and Schuster, 1997), 1518.

Chapter 33: Birthday Joy

1. Walt Whitman, "O Me! O Life!" in *Leaves of Grass* (Philadelphia, 1892).

Chapter 34: In Sunsets

1. Frederick Buechner, *The Hungering Dark* (HarperCollins, 1969), 75.

Chapter 35: In the Face of Death

1. Philippians 4:4
2. Acts 8:1
3. Acts 9:1–2
4. Acts 9:15–16
5. Acts 27:44
6. Philippians 1:12
7. Philippians 1:14
8. Philippians 1:20
9. Philippians 1:28
10. Philippians 1:4
11. Philippians 1:18
12. Philippians 2:29
13. Philippians 2:1–2

14. Philippians 2:6–8
15. Philippians 2:14
16. Philippians 3:5
17. Philippians 3:9
18. Philippians 4:7
19. Philippians 1:21

Chapter 36: Don't Be Such a Pollyanna!

1. Eleanor H. Porter, *Pollyanna* (Independently Published, 2022), 34.
2. Porter, *Pollyanna*, 63.
3. Porter, *Pollyanna*, 95.
4. Porter, *Pollyanna*, 96–97.
5. James 1:2–3